MW00427454

THINK RIGHT

FOR

HEALTH AND SUCCESS

BY

GRACE M. BROWN
AUTHOR OF MENTAL HARMONY, ETC.

NEW YORK
EDWARD J. CLODE
PUBLISHER

THINK RIGHT

Human Measurement

THE human being is created in the image and likeness of God.

That statement alone if truly realized and really accepted would solve the human problem, because it would adjust the man in perfect mathematical relation to the divine part of himself and so prove his unity with God.

It would free you and me from untold confusion and anguish by relating us to our own responsibility and proving to us most positively that:

We have no right to be sick.

We have no right to be poor.

We have no right to be sorrowful.

And, mightier than all, it would free us from the agony of separation by the present form of death, because the glorious God of whom we are a part, in whom we live and move and have our being, cannot die and we are created in the image and likeness of the imperishable and ever living God.

The individual being made in the image of God has the divine attribute of will and the consequent power of selection; also the universe is in process and the individual is in process; the individual is the microcosm of the universe and the universe is not yet perfect, and in the journey toward ultimate completeness there are many experiences.

When the man forgets his responsibility to and in and with himself, he also forgets his relation to God and the allness of God — so he misdirects his divine power of being good and being complete which results in being healthy and happy — and in the misdirection of his goodness he causes an inaccuracy of action which results in a lack of good, and all lack of good causes pain on some plane of expression, whether it be of the flesh or of supply or some other condition.

All untruth to ourselves is unfaith toward God, and in our falsity to ourselves and our faithlessness to God and to each other we cause more and more of separation, more and more of misunderstanding, until it seems to our human conception that the light of truth has gone out and that we are submerged in the anguish of unbelief.

Every disease of the flesh is caused by some process of mental action which relates the thinker to the lack or to the reverse action of some divine force, and the healing of that form of disease must come from the plane of its expression. Fear thoughts attract to the thinker anything upon which he centers his attention; "the thing you fear will come upon you," and being the opposite pole of faith, Faith is the force to use in dissolving the confusion generated by Fear.

In like manner diseases caused by hate and condemnation and all repelling forces must be dissolved by the applied force of its opposite pole of love, in creative action with faith, which render all destructive operation void; and it is so in all phases and forms of disease — they are healed by the same force in constructive action which generated them in destructive action.

Faith is a divine force — an attribute of God, as it were; it is an actual substance which proves its actualness whenever you formulate it in your mind and utilize your thought force in bringing it into action.

Fear is the reverse activity of faith. They two are the same magnetic force in different rates of vibration, Faith being the force in the rapid action of good which vibrates co-operatively and coherently and constructively with God, and Fear being the same force in a negative vibration which disconnects and disrupts and works destructively because of its lack of co-operation with good.

You can only attract and assimilate thought forces which are of your own quality and you can only attract as much of the universal thought energy as you have the capacity to assimilate — otherwise you might attract by and through your own fear enough of destructive energy to disintegrate your flesh form at once.

In all healing work the process must be on the plane of its own action: if you are using the material and medical process you will use material remedies; if you are using the mental process you will use the mind forces; and if your process is purely spiritual you will use spiritual forces.

But, whatever your process, your medium for action and consequent expression will be the mind, because you cannot think outside of mind — you cannot comprehend or live coherently apart from mind; it is the medium of all present consciousness of being and of action.

Should you realize that you have devitalized and distorted your portion of God's life and are manifesting your life in pain or in poverty or grief, you may also realize that you have the divine right and the consequent power to reconstruct yourself and so balance yourself in your own accurate position in the universe.

Opulent balanced life action relates us to God — the all good — and it is our privilege, yours and mine, to attract and to express the opulence of God's great goodness on any and all planes of our being, and in order to do so we will learn to think coherently and form our own point of view, our own angle, concerning the things which relate to the mastery and the reconstruction of ourselves and our conditions.

Too long has the individual forgotten his individuality and his unity with God; too long has he been a servant and a slave of opinion; and a thousand times too long has he lived his life from the vision of others and accepted disease and poverty in the distorted belief that it was the will of God; and he has actually worshiped a God who he believed had unjustly scourged and whom he fully expected to cast him into an after-death hell for pure revenge after he had held him for years in a present-day hell upon this fair earth home.

Glory be to the oncoming, onrushing force of the mighty truth of God's allness! The present-day hell is dissolving fast, and the light of heaven is already enfolding the chil-

dren of the ever-living and all-powerful and,
greater than all else, the ever-loving God.

Every atom of substance, whether expressed
or unexpressed, is spirit substance, and mind is
the medium which, according to its vibratory
force and the quality of the intention back of
that force, produces all effect and all manifestation from and of the great primal substance and its active cause in mind.

Thought is mind in action, therefore.
Thought is the conscious formulated energy
emanating from mind which is responsible
for all human as well as all universal manifestation — and as it is the human being we
are studying to-day we will analyze a few ideas
concerning human thought.

Now this human being, created in the
image and likeness of God, has in himself
all of the universal possibility and all the
divine attributes of the infinite intelligence
and he will externalize all of Godness and
master himself by knowing himself.

And the man will know himself by desiring
to know himself.

You and I have arrived at the point of our human progress where we desire to know ourselves, and first and foremost we are discovering that in order to know ourselves we must learn to think; that is, we must use our minds in coherent action; otherwise our part of the infinite mind may use us incoherently, because it is our responsibility, as we are part of the universal expression, to use our portion of life and intelligence according to our capacity, which means according to the best we know, for responsibility is merely responding to truth with the best of our human ability.

With the intention to think coherently, to use our minds or rather our part of the infinite mind according to our own desire and inspiration, we commence to realize something of our relation to the universe — in other words, the relation of the human to the divine and of the finite to the infinite — and then we perceive that thought is our material, and the part of it which we select is our capital for our entire life action; also that we may do what we will to do with our own capital.

In the studying of ourselves we naturally analyze ourselves, and in the analysis we recognize our power, and in that recognition our capacity increases and we find ourselves steadily and surely becoming masters of our thought, and in that vital mastery we are uplifting ourselves and consequently the entire race.

All accomplishment comes, first, by attracting the thought energy with discrimination; second, by assimilating it in love; third, by wisely expending it.

It rests entirely with you and me what quality of thought energy we will entertain; we naturally attract thoughts which are of our own quality, but we need not retain any form of the universal energy with which we have finished and for which we have no use.

The man becomes what his thoughts represent. If they are constructively relating and attaching him to the life current, his force is everlasting and his existence is eternal. If, on the contrary, his thoughts are destructive and therefore disintegrating, his soul has not the necessary co-operation for its expression and dissolution on some plane, usually of the flesh form, results.

Men may have as much as they will use and no more of the grand universal current of thought energy — and using means giving according to the best of our capacity in order that the capacity may strengthen to receive more and more of the opulence of the infinite love and wisdom.

Every thought which is attracted and assimilated and sent out by the individual carries with it a suggestion, and whoever and whatever is of its quality is on the line of that suggestion.

Possibly some of you may remember that the epidemic of la grippe was introduced into America by a cablegram which was published in the newspapers, and, even when not published, epidemics of constructive conditions as well as destructive have manifested themselves through mental suggestion.

When the mind is not trained and the thinker is destructive in his consciousness, that is, when he is afraid or angry or otherwise confused, the thought has less power and is more easily dissolved, but the power of a thought formulated by a trained mind, and directed with the accuracy which belongs to the intelligent master of a trained mind, cannot be overestimated — not because of its present power, but because, being on an orderly and a constructive basis, it endures for always.

Which is the reason that one constructive thinker is more powerful than thousands of destructive ones — verily the gates of hell cannot prevail against him. Were it not so, the planet itself would dissolve in the confusion of its myriads of destructive thinkers who, even now, in this supposedly enlightened time, are shrieking for each other's blood and are groveling and grafting and selling their souls for each other's possessions.

Thoughts which are based upon falsity, such as fear and hate and condemnation, are not enduring; they perish by the weight of their own delusion and they are impotent in their falsity, because the life current is pure

and undying truth, and no thing and no force
can long endure against its living accuracy.

While truth in its entirety never changes
and its principles are immune, each mind perceives it from a different angle and consequently each vision varies.

Few people, however, have the courage to
be sufficiently true to themselves to live from
their own angle of vision; they have not yet
become individual, and so when a man formulates a broader conception of truth than
his fellow-men, it places him a trifle apart and
others look askance and declare that such an
intrusion of ideas beyond their own may
mean change and better be suppressed.

So for many ages has it been with the form
of truth which deals with the spiritual healing of the flesh form through the medium of
the mind; there have always been, as there
are now, those who have preferred to endure
the anguish of flesh dissolution through the
disease process rather than to accept a truth
by and through an apparent mystery.

And as the human creature is free, it is his

privilege to suffer and to die if he wants that
experience — it is his divine right to select his
part of the great spirit substance and equally
his divine right to manipulate it and direct it
in response to his own desire.

Now we have decreed, you and I, that we
will use our freedom by freeing ourselves and
we cannot be free with our bodies in the
bondage of pain and in harmony. So we are
going to forgive and to forget all of our past
suffering and discord and we shall stop our
habit of thinking at random and allow other
people's thoughts to control us; instead, we
shall balance our own minds and so regulate
our own thought energy.

Therein lies the first step toward becoming spiritual in our flesh forms and of purify-
ing every atom of them and healing every
inequality that they may become whole in
the consciousness of the wholeness or holiness
of infinite life.

The first conscious effort in the direction of
mind mastery is the process of intelligently
centering the thought force with formulated

intention; this process is ofttimes called concentration or centering the thought, and in order to center the thought one must give it his undivided attention.

The triangle of concentration is Attention, Contemplation, and Meditation.

Attention steadies the mind and attracts the chosen thought; Contemplation fixes and establishes the thought in the mind and adjusts it to the present condition and requirement.

Contemplation is upon the plane of reason; it argues and balances and adjusts, it analyzes and regulates and decides — then, having formulated a decision through its own balancing force, Meditation naturally follows and the student enters upon a plane of conscious and cosmic understanding which relates him to knowledge.

. . .

The sort of knowledge which we are claiming to-day is that which gives us the ability to control our physical bodies and to relate them to perfect health, and the same quality of knowledge enables us also to control our environment and our bank account, because the interpenetrating force of the finer forces of nature — the more spiritual force, as it were — brings balance in the all good to all which it may contact.

These finer forces of nature, such as Faith and Love and Hope and Courage, etc., etc., operate upon the finite being through the medium of finite mind; so we will realize that our human or finite mind is a measured portion of the divine or infinite mind, in fact that it is the infinite mind expressing itself in finite form, wherein it is measured and limited or extended according to our capacity or, in more accurate wording, according to our conception of ourselves.

Thus the human mind has the same attributes and the same privileges as the infinite mind, because it is a portion of that mind and its difference in power is only in the degree of its intentive force.

In order to relate our finite minds to a comprehension of infinite mind, let us place our thought upon the primal substance of spirit and then let us know that every atom in the universe is an intelligent atom and that whatever its present form, it is fundamentally and primarily pure spirit substance.

Following that idea, let us adjust our mind action, which is our thought, in direct line with the thought or the mind action of the infinite intelligence, with the awareness of our unity with it or, in other words, with the consciousness that we are one and a part of that intelligence in all of its activity, and that it is therefore, our responsibility to do our part, in the mental control and manipulation of the formless spirit substance in bringing it into the manifestation, through orderly energy, of orderly form.

Nothing gives us a firmer grasp upon our own power than this clear vision of the infinite unity of universal life and consequently of our own part in and with it: therein we see our greatness, because we see the greatness of God and all that lives and moves and is of Him.

Suppose we are not using our thought force intelligently — that is, suppose we are, through our own ignorance, which is merely ignoring the law of our own life, not doing our part in the constructive and orderly adjustment of the universal manifestation and are, therefore, expressing destruction and disease, shall we despair and grieve and feel that life here is over for us?

No, indeed, unless we desire to leave the planet by such a destructive route. There is always the opportunity of a mighty recall; a recall of repentance which completely reverses the forces of destruction and merges their activity in the constructive operation of God wherein we may, even with our finite consciousness, reconstruct and readjust and heal all that is in disorder and confused suffering by and through our reconnection with God's mighty love and supreme wisdom.

We do not make statements which cannot be definitely explained and positively proven, and we have said and are proving it factual that there is a method and a process for every

accomplishment on every plane of life concerning which we have the capacity to formulate thought. Also it is true that no
demand can be made upon us which we have
not made possible by our desire, and the
process may always be discovered through the
understanding of the desire.

Many times it appears that we are not quite
equal to the thing we have assumed, that our
burden is greater than we, and that we shall
be submerged under its great weight.

It is not true. The fact that we assumed
it proves positively that we desired it, and
that it remains with us is a definite assur-
ance that its quality is of our own or it could
not remain.

When we grow greater than our problem,
stronger than our burden through the greatness of our wisdom and the strength of our
love, all of confusion will utterly dissolve,
because in the dynamic action of love and
wisdom in co-operation no thing destructive
can possibly endure.

Thinking constructively means thinking

always the uplifting thought concerning yourself and everybody else; it means realizing
the love nature and the love quality of every
living creature; it means knowing that everything manifest is of God whether or not its
immediate expression is Godlike.

Thinking constructively is not thinking spas-
modically, with a love thought one moment
and a fear thought the next — with a thought
of hope and divine intention to-day and a
fall into despair to-morrow: that process of
mind action is most confusing, because, being
uncertain, the result is unexpected and unequal to the mental atmospheric conditions
and conflict is sure to follow.

In the recognition and the realization of
the good and only the good in all of intelligent action, you have the appreciation and
respect of yourself, which is a most potent
healing force; indeed very much of disease
is caused by regret and self-condemnation —
and you also have a spiritual stimulant for
all of your life's intention. And really it
matters very little what are the opinions of

other people concerning you so long as you have your own love and appreciation for yourself — but that is absolutely essential if you would be true to yourself and if you intend to accomplish your part toward the completeness of the planet you have selected for your present abiding place.

And one vital part of your work upon this earth home is that you adjust your physical flesh form in complete and balanced expression here and now.

You may have been told that you are controlled by the planets — indeed some systems of philosophy are bounded north, east, south, and west by the belief in Zodiacal limitations; they evidently do not perceive that the creature that is made in the image of God is far greater than any such, or indeed any limitation, because the finite mind being a measured portion of the infinite mind is of universal or cosmic quality and can dominate and sweep infinite and cosmic realms instead of being ruled by the conditions of one little solar system.

Naturally so long as we make it our abiding place, we are more or less influenced by the conditions of this solar system, just as we are influenced by the climatic conditions of the earth while we are breathing its atmosphere.

When we know the truth of a fact or a condition — not only believe it but actually know it — we also know how to meet it and, if necessary, how to overcome it. When it is cold to the point of discomfort, we are sufficiently wise to create heat. Likewise we are great enough to ride the waters and to bend their mighty power to our service, also to utilize the forces of the fire and the earth and the air in response to our human desire and intention.

Therefore, shall we, you and I, allow these finer forces of life to turn upon us and rend us, as it were, when we have within us all that is greater than they and when we can bend them to our intention and utililize them for our ever-increasing strength and glory?

Verily nothing can intrude upon us and nothing can glorify us but ourselves.

We have decreed that we shall manifest health and opulence on each and every plane of our being; so we will immediately commence to think opulently. We will think concerning the fullness in consciousness that there is such mighty abundance in the universe that it is more than equal for all the life forms within it — more than all the human claim which can possibly be made upon it; there is always the supply to meet every demand, and if we strengthen our demand, naturally the supply strengthens and increases in abundance.

Abundance of health — such marvelous abundance.

Freedom and fullness in and of every requirement conceivable to the human mind.

We glory in the treasures in our Father's house, in our home; we glory in the many mansions, in our especial mansion; and we claim our birthright of health and of prosperity, of beauty and of joy.

Do you think any sort of poverty — of the body or the mind or the purse — can long exist in an atmosphere created by such a vitalized dynamic thought as that?

Hold fast to the idea of your own greatness — it is such a marvelous tonic — and cling with the faith of eternity to God's greatness that no lesser thought may come between you and your faith in yourself.

You will find the mantrims below of value in flesh healing — their cadence is such that they interpenetrate with dynamic accuracy.

Memorize them — commit them to consciousness and you will perceive their effect when you need the surcharge of a positive reconstructive energy.

There are several here given, because different conditions may demand a different tone, and there are many conditions and many tones.

And remember always and always, whatever the need, whatever the response, there is only good, for God is all and there is nothing else beside.

The light of God's love shineth forever.

Its radiance is as the encircling glory of a

mighty sun which dissolves the night shadows and reveals the oncoming day.

Behold, I place myself within its rising glow and I breathe its flaming energy in and through every atom of my flesh form.

I am ashine with the light of truth.

I am aflame with the glow of health.

I am enriched with divine abundance.

I am free in the knowledge that I am at-one with God.

My body is the temple of my soul: it shall be clean.

My body is the externalization of my thought: it shall be whole.

My body is the manifestation of my intention: it shall be beautiful.

For my flesh is to my mind as the clay in the artist's hand; it reflects the genius and the love of me.

. .

Come, Lord of life, let thy glory enfold this, our earth home, that the black night of disease may dissolve from this fair realm and that sin and death may be no more.

Come, gracious Father, and fill the flesh of man with the radiance of thy truth, that life itself may reign supreme and that mankind may be free to serve Thee and only Thee.

Verily the fullness of the earth is God, for all goodness is of Him.

The love of God is the heart of wisdom, and in His love and wisdom is knowledge, the all-knowledge of Being and action, the mighty knowledge which passeth all understanding.

Know thyself in Him, O man, and knowing thyself thou shalt be whole in His holy name.

• . •

The light shineth ever.

The light dissolves all of darkness.

The light reveals, ay, it is the presence of the ever-living God, and in His presence there is perfect health and perfect joy.

Arise, O Man, and declare for thine own path in freedom, that it may lead thee to the light of God's presence, which absolves thee from all pain and all woe.

Love is the joy of the world.

Love heals the sick and strengthens the weary.

Love frees the grief burdened; love endureth forever.

Love is all and gives all yet love, true love, makes no claim; it is greater than all claim and beyond all limitation.

. .

In the beginning was God —
Now is God.
In the future shall be God.
For He is all
And there is naught beside.

STUDY OF COMMON SENSE
SPIRITUALITY

I have learned that when I am kind to life that life is kind to me.

I have learned that the responsibility of my part of life is to give all that I have and all that I am and all that I know, freely and unreservedly to those who need it, with no thought of result and no expectation of reward.

I have learned that when I do the very best I know at all times and in all ways that the greatest things I am capable of knowing are added unto me.

I have learned these facts by accepting the privilege of my human individuality and using my common sense.

Study of Common Sense Spirituality

The thing that divides is satanic,
The thing that unites is divine.
The thought that decrees is dynamic,
The force that creates is sublime.

UMANITY is composed of many human beings who are working in togetherness for the common completeness of the whole race.

God is made manifest in humanity through the good in the common activity of that humanity.

Common sense applies spiritual balance to the natural things of everyday life; it is, as it were, the voice of one crying in our human wilderness preparing us to meet the law of our human life in love and in wisdom.

Common sense gives a polarized and therefore intelligent vision whereby the soul can operate through its bodily instrument for the all-good in its earth manifestation and so prepare for its life and work in other realms.

We are here upon the earth home, living its common everyday experiences, because we require just this place and just these experiences, for our own good, which means for our own relinquishment of self and our consequent revealment of God.

Not one of us differs greatly from the other — we are all manifesting in clay bodies because we have all selected the clay planet for our present abiding place, and we could not vibrate in its key where we not of its texture and equipped for its life expression and thereby enabled to breathe its atmosphere.

Common sense relates us to our humanly intelligent as well as to our divinely intelligent requirement; it inspires us to adjust ourselves to and with our claims and their responsibilities both here and in the beyond phases of our lives and to recognize our necessities both of the flesh and of the spirit, that they may be fulfilled.

Our clay bodies are well equipped, in fact much better equipped than most of us realize; we only know of five senses, but there are

many times five senses in these flesh forms
and we shall soon awaken to perceive them,
As a race we are awakening to the sense of
intuition which forms an immediate connection between the human and the divine of
us and as individuals we are commencing to
realize and recognize it and so strengthen it,
but we are so closely related that we must
all awaken before the individual can really be
aware of the truth of his God power.

While jealousy runs riot in one human
mind, all humanity suffers therefrom.

While legalized murder sweeps part of the
earth and mows down many of God's images
in ignorant frenzy, all men shall suffer —
otherwise they would not be as one in infinite
life and love.

And we are commonly one in our humanity
as we are children of the divine household of
our Father in Heaven and one in His home.

In the ordinary terminology common sense
is supposed to apply to those things known
as material but the material things, the
every-day essences and activities of our lives

are quite as spiritual as other forces yet untouched and therefore called mysterious.

Common sense dissolves mystery by relating it to reason.

The finer forces of life interpenetrate the coarser, thereby refining the whole, and these common activities of daily living need to be interpenetrated by the finer, but quite as common, forces in nature in order that they may more accurately balance in the doing of their perfect work.

The human creature causes some vast mishappenings by his misconception of relationship; he needs to bring God into his daily commonplace expression, he needs the divine association in his eating and in his sleeping, in his living and in his dying — he needs to know daily and hourly the commonplace fact of the presence of the ever-living, everloving God, and his common sense will reveal to him that only in that divine intimacy will his humanity become aware of its pure goodness.

There is no problem in Life's vast variety

which may not be met and solved in the light
of a spiritual vision balanced by common sense;
one need not be limited ever so slightly if he
will use his common sense in everything that
he does and says.

The claim of growing beyond human requirement and earthly method belongs to the
early stages of fanaticism and is entirely apart
from common sense and its balanced reason;
indeed, if a soul had grown beyond human
need while yet upon the earth planet, he
would have common sense enough not to
mention it.

The great limitation of the human race is
fear; men are afraid of each other because
they are afraid of themselves, and in their
fear emotion they demagnetize their bodies
and every condition which concerns their part
of life.

Common sense comes to the rescue and says
there is absolutely nothing to fear; in its
balanced light you see that by being afraid
you attract the mighty destroyer, emotion,
upon you, and it proves to you that emotion

is a most confusing force which acts as a blur and a blight upon every thought form which it touches.

Emotion feeds upon disaster and thrives upon grief, and it is quite time that the human creature steadies his mind and balances himself in a common sense spirituality wherein he can abide and strengthen his capacity for attracting and assimilating the infinite good which he claims.

Life is not a joke and we are not here only to have fun — we are here to bring our part of life to the highest form of its expression which we have selected and which we have the capacity to meet, and it is our privilege, which is but another word for duty, to constantly and consistently strengthen our capacity.

Naturally we shall create harmony by so doing and happiness will result, but happiness is not hysterical fun — neither is it resultant from emotion of any kind; it is consistent and enduring harmony made manifest in daily living.

When humanity commences to use its common sense, it will recognize its individuality, and there is no vitalized accomplishment until the man realizes his power by realizing his individuality.

In the vast unity of the human race, each atom must stand out accurately as a vitalized unit so that the whole may be perfect and so unified, and in order to become so polarized we must know that every other soul has as definite a place and as important a work as we.

Therefore we will agree in our intention to know God and we will glorify our introspective vision by viewing our brother's part of life from his angle of vision. Nothing will so equalize our own life action as to recognize every other human creature as equal with us and as worthy of the same privileges which we claim for ourselves.

Most people think entirely from their own angle, and it is too often a limited and narrow line of vision, not extending out of their immediate circle; when they commence to glimpse a realm beyond their own, they are quite likely to feel the impulse to investigate the farther glimpse, and when they do investigate and breathe the broader atmosphere, as it were, their cosmic unfoldment has commenced.

It is then that the human creature needs his common sense; he wants to grow, and mayhap he has not yet discovered that growth is not a comfortable process and that the entrance to any new realm causes suffering and travail until we have grown so universally conscious that we are unified with all realms; possibly then the man resents the discomfort of the process which leads him to the thing he has claimed, and resentment may darken his way and retard his journey toward his Father's home, which is the universal and infinite realm.

No other soul can live for us, and no other soul can die for us, but we can all inspire each other to take the step in consciousness which will render us each greater than the problem

we have undertaken to solve and make us
equal to the mastery of our own part of God's
great life.

Some day soon, please heaven, all this wo-
ful misunderstanding with its agonizing result
shall pass away; men will look into each
other's eyes and see the God therein, and in
that divinely glorified vision we shall know
each other as we are, without the crust of
delusion and the heartache of fear; we shall
know that each man and each woman is just
exactly what the person who loves him and
her best believes them to be, and we shall
trust each other in the consciousness of that
satisfying truth which is the evidence of God
because it results from the sure knowledge of
good.

No matter how enigmatical a statement
may appear, just analyze it in the light of
your common sense, and you will soon know
whether or not it is worthy of your concentration and so qualify your flesh atoms with
it — for common sense is the universal rea-
soner; it sifts the wheat from the chaff and

actually relates the human creature to his own part of life.

Herein I give you a few statements for study and practise.

Do not accept them because I have found them useful; the thing which may be a definite power for my polarization may not belong to you at all.

It is for you to turn the light into your own consciousness, decide for your own good, and let no human opinion swerve you from that which you know is your own.

To-day is the day of my salvation.

To-day I claim that I am love.

I am one with all love, and the light of love is wisdom.

Love gives thanks that this is the day of salvation.

Love knows that humanity is free from sin, sickness, sorrow, poverty, and death.

Love is waiting to enfold every living creature who will accept its glorifying radiance.

Love makes no demand; it only knows its own. Love asks no favors; it only seeks to be, — for in love's being all is given and received, and in love's freedom all life's gracious gifts are unreserved.

Love is the most practical of nature's finer forces, because it is all-inclusive and all-harmonious with every quality of good: it vibrates in the key of good, so it becomes all-attractive to the good things of life, and success on every plane breathes in its atmosphere.

The man who loves his work is he who succeeds.

The woman who loves her home glorifies it, and her husband is not interested in the news of the divorce court.

One might continue indefinitely to cite cases of the practical effect of love in its everyday common sense activity because health and happiness and riches and every condition that makes life worth while abide in its atmosphere.

Let us sing the song of that everyday common sense love which simply is because we open our hearts to admit it, and so it enters into our flesh forms, rendering us a glorified expression of life.

In the shine of the love light all that seems distorted is made plain.

And the darkness melts into day.

The accurate process of living is the simplest and the most natural, and there is no escaping the fact that we cannot swerve from the accurate angle of expression and not suffer: that is why it is the common sense process to open our hearts to love because love is natural and accurate, knowing no evil and consequently attracting no pain.

When we lessen our ability to naturally love, we also lessen our power to accurately live, and thereby we place the joys of life farther and farther away from our part of life and misunderstanding follows, and in the misdirection of forces which follow the shadows perplexingly fall.

It is common sense to live because you love to live.

It is common sense to work because you love to work and to play because you love to play, for the reason that your life and your work and your play are only successful in the love vibration.

It is common sense to pray to your heavenly Father that you may abide in togetherness with Him where life itself becomes one glorious revelation of His love.

. .

Father of all that lives and moves,
Father of all that feels and knows,
Manifestor of stars and suns,
Creator of worlds and worlds;
I AM Thy child,
Heart of Thy heart,
Mind of Thy mind,
Soul of Thy soul,
Breath of Thy breath
And one with Thy life.

Can you not see in the blowing breeze,
In the dancing leaves on their parent trees,
In the blossoming bud all blushing and sweet
As it opens its heart the sunlight to greet,
The handiwork of God?

Can you not feel in the silent sweep
Of nature's awaking from ages of sleep,
In the wonderful reach toward infinite things
And the answer to needs which each day brings,
That He is aware?

Do you not know that the vivid gleam
Enfolding the earth with its radiant beam,
Filling with love all pulsing life,
Freeing mankind from its fear and its strife,
Is God's own truth?

Oh, marvelous Truth of infinite power,
Rising supreme each day and each hour,
No life can endure apart from Thee,
No love can exist that is not free
In Thy great name.

STUDY CONCERNING THOUGHT

"Think," said the Lord of Heaven
To the waking, breathing spark,
THINK thyself into living,
THINK thyself into loving,
THINK thyself into God's light!
And out of the creeping dark.

Study Concerning Thought

HOUGHT is the conscious, formulated motive energy of the primal substance.

Thought invariably precedes action, being the intentive force of all action and all manifestation.

The formation of thought force and its resultant activity is based upon a principle which is as factual as mathematical law, and there is no compromise with mathematical law, so truth, which is the accurate action of the law and the evidence of good, is the thought manifestation of a definite principle which must stand every possible test of reason and analysis.

A philosophy to have endurance is founded upon truth, and must follow in its development the principles of this truth law; otherwise it cannot be constructive in its teaching and influence, because there can be no chaotic imaginings and no weird calculations in a process of thought which is based upon the life principle of enduring truth.

Thought does not relate alone to human mental action.

Thought is the universal current of consciousness, and so it is a universal force pertaining to the universal and infinite mind.

Thought becomes a human expression of consciousness in degree as the human being responds and relates himself to universal consciousness.

As the human creature becomes more and more aware of his relation to the universe — in other words, of the relation of the human to the divine — he commences to interpret this thought force and to realize that it is his capital for his entire life action and that he may do what we wills to do with this wonderful and unlimited material.

When the man perceives his power in and of thinking, he then commences to study himself, and the more he analyzes himself from his own life angle, the more he realizes

that there is a mighty force within himself
which is the living motive energy in his life
action.

Recognition of ability means a strengthening capacity for all of life's operations, and it
rests with the man whether he will recognize
and appreciate himself and so become a power
for good for himself and for his race or whether
he will ignore his opportunity and fail to use
his divine ability.

The human creature is not a creation of
circumstance; rather he is a creation of his
own intention and his own love desire in
using that intention.

There is one universal current of mind
action which produces what we call thought
energy, and men may have as much of that
thought energy as they will use and no more,
and using means giving to life according to
their individual capacity in order that their
capacity may strengthen and enable them
to receive more.

All accomplishment comes first by recognizing the thought energy, second by attract-

ing it, third by assimilating it, and fourth by wisely expending it.

To be sure, very few of us comprehend the process of our unfoldment until we are on a conscious plane of evolution, but the process is there whether we are aware of it or not.

The rose blooms in all its glory through and by its own power of externalizing the thought energy which it has attracted and assimilated and used according to its strength and its quality, but it is not conscious of its process any more than is the bird aware of the marvelous intelligence which enables it to fly.

The human creature, however, is the microcosm of the universe; he has evolved to the place where he is made in the image of God, body, mind, and soul; he is a part of that infinite intelligence through which he lives and moves and has his being; he has the divine attributes and he may think in the universal key whenever he so decrees.

The phase of thought energy with which the human being must deal is that of individual thought control, because it rests entirely with the man what quality of thought energy he will entertain. He naturally attracts thoughts which are responsive to his own quality, but he need not retain or entertain any form of the universal energy which is not responsive to his will.

Every thought formulated by the will and sent out from the individual mind is a suggestion of some sort; even if not directed toward any special person, it may seriously affect some one who has not yet learned the law of mental self-protection and who is especially sensitive to that quality of thought.

The power of a thought formulated by a trained mind and directed with the accuracy and intelligence of that mind is most dynamic, not only because of its immediate strength, but because its intentive force endures forever.

The man becomes the thing concerning which he thinks and which he thereby breathes into himself; he may be whatever he desires to be, he may live the life he selects, he may have what his love demands — if he will only be true to the God of himself and think good.

All thinking which is built upon negative or destructive lines, such as fear, condemnation, resentment, or any other disorderly formulation, does not endure, because the life current moves in exact accordance with the law which is the mathematical activity of its motion.

Therefore the life current is truth itself in its action, and nothing can prevail against it; any attempt to do so always results in disorders of flesh or mind or purse.

Men in their present limited consciousness do not readily respond to a different or newer expression of thought; it requires mental effort to change one's viewpoint; it might change one's relation to life, and few human creatures are willing to think for themselves; it is much easier to have some one else solve their problems and to go along life's pathway in the same rut other rut-lovers have trod, and so they prefer the vicarious method, not even permitting themselves to think seriously concerning it or they would realize that it is utterly impractical.

Each soul must think for himself and solve his own problems of life and death or they will not be solved.

Truth, being the result of mathematical action of the life energy, has an infinite variety of expression; each externalized form, each life manifestation, results from the truth thought of an infinite intelligence.

Every and each human mind, from the angle of its position and according to its relation with this infinite intelligence, sees life and truth from its viewpoint, and each vision naturally varies. It has happened that some of the earth children have insisted that other of the earth children think from their angle of vision, and they who were strongest compelled, and so we have slaves and tyrants on many planes of our life manifestation.

When a man takes a step in advance of his fellows by formulating a broader idea of truth or any of its myriads of attributes, it places him somewhat apart from them in consciousness, and sometimes they feel uncomfortable about such an intrusion of advancing thought

and demand that he and his new idea shall
be suppressed.

It is not long since Mesmer, with his giant
mind, undertook to prove by actual illustra-
tion of fact that he had discovered a method
of controlling thought energy and of utiliz-
ing that energy. Certain people declared that
he was crazy, and even now the term "mes-
merism," and its accompanying word "hypnotism," is spoken by many with almost a feeling
of dread.

And yet the force applied in the simplest
of life regulations is frequently the same
force which, if labeled correctly, would be
called hypnotism. We hypnotize ourselves
when we put ourselves to sleep. The
mother hypnotizes her child when she sug-
gests and controls by her mental suggestion
his action.

In the business world, men do not engage
in a hand-to-hand encounter; it is a thought-
to-thought encounter, and, with mind pitted
against mind, men meet and greet and part
and meet again, and the master mind, the

one which thinks more rapidly, wins in each encounter.

If men were conscious of the process of their mind action they would be masters of it.

If men were masters of their mind action, they would know how to think.

If men knew how to think, they would control their bodies and their life conditions, and there could be no lack of physical or financial strength.

The fact is that it is stupid to live a life of negative intention — in other words, to be resigned to poverty on any plane, and most people accept conditions negatively; they do not retain or use the thoughts they attract, otherwise the world would not be in the throes of despair as it is to-day.

The world needs thinkers, people who dare to view life from their angle in the universe and who have the strength to live their part of the universal life in the line of their vision of truth.

Such people, those who are true to themselves and their convictions, are always true

to every other earth creature, because the
soul who lives in his own truth angle knows
that he and all of God's creatures are one in
their interest and their work of the earth life
expression.

. . .

The finite mind, being a measured portion
of the infinite mind, is measured and limited
according to the individual capacity, or it
might be more accurate to say according to
the man's conception of himself.

Therefore the human mind differs from the
universal mind only in degree; it has the same
attributes, the same privileges, and is of the
same quality.

The human mind has the divine capacity
of development, and when it understands that
it has the power of mastering its thought action and consequently its life externalization,
the development of the individual becomes
certain and rapid.

When men know this truth of themselves
and thereby the truth of each other, they
will not be divided against each other, because

they will know that such division means the destruction of flesh and strength and love.

The song of ages is that men become exactly what they think, and had it not been true the song would have died out long ago; all philosophers, all teachers, and indeed all thinkers have so proclaimed, and yet we see on every hand withering flesh, distorted homes, poverty and its accompanying anguish, all because men are too indolent to think themselves into life and freedom.

A man cannot think concerning anything which is not in and of himself; if he thinks concerning God, it is because there is good in himself; if he forgets to think of God, he is weakening the real of himself and making the way plain for disorder to possess him.

The broader and freer the individual thought becomes, the greater and more good becomes the individual; he is on the true road toward universal consciousness when he allows himself to think universally and not limit himself to a small corner of his own finite realm.

When the soul assumes the responsibility of its humanity, it also assumes the responsibility of glorifying that humanity and rendering it worthy of its divine relationship.

Consequently, human creatures have no right to use their part of the thought energy in destruction, and when they do, in their own flesh is made manifest any violation of God's law.

So long as men believe that they cannot control their thoughts or that they must think what other people have thought and found suitable for them, so long they will be unable to control their life conditions.

It is for the individual to think what he wills to think, and then he will do what he intends to do.

It is wise, it is practical, indeed it is essential, that we always think good of ourselves; in the first place, it is the only way we can think good of other folks; also it relates the atoms of our flesh body to strength, because we breathe into our flesh the thoughts which we select to entertain.

Sometimes we select to entertain thoughts which act like a great stupefying force and which result in arrested development on certain planes of our life externalization; then we have an unequal or unbalanced condition which is not strengthening to our health either of body or of purse.

Men are, in truth, always good, but they do not always know it, and not knowing it they have not the power to think their goodness into themselves.

There are many voices crying in the wilderness, many souls suffering from the ache of their hearts and, perhaps, from the awfulness of sickness and poverty and from the thing which men call sin.

Verily, they know that the prophet is at hand, but they scarcely dare think of the new prophet, which is a mighty principle of life, when there are so many personal prophets encrusted by opinion and forced upon their attention.

God help and bless them, few people yet know that the light is always shining which

utterly dissolves the crust of misery which
humanity has been accumulating for so many
ages.

And blessed souls, how can they understand,
when they will not think, that they themselves darken its shine by their own super-
stition?

O man, can you not see that it is easy to
enter into the light of truth in freedom by
realizing the God of yourself?

Your concern is with and for yourself; it
is not for you to think for your fellow-man
until you have thought yourself into love for
him.

It is time to think concerning God and his
great goodness, that our love shall be unwaver-
ing and that we may dissolve every condition
of confusion which overshadows the world.

STUDY CONCERNING FREEDOM

My blessed Lord,
I know that thou and I are one,
Then why despair —

Beloved Truth,
All life apart from thee I shun
And I declare —

That I am free in Truth's own name,
That life is mine to hold and claim,
That I shall work with highest aim
For God's great Truth
In Freedom's name.

Study Concerning Freedom

NO word of human tongues is so mis-understood as the word "freedom."

No force of all the finer forces of nature is more incomprehensible to men than the force of freedom.

Of all the God gifts, men most desire what they call freedom, when in truth it is the one thing they utterly refuse to allow entrance into their mental realm.

The man prays for freedom; he longs for his idea of freedom because the thing men call freedom is to do as they please from the narrow angle of their earth vision, and too often it is merely the limited glimpse of their earth desire.

. .

Suppose we analyze this evanescent, chaste force of freedom. Let us use our spiritual Calculus and see if we can relate ourselves to its clear potent energy and perhaps comprehend in some degree its truth quality.

Truth is always the evidence of good, and it represents the balance action of all of the finer forces of nature.

Truth only operates in freedom, which is the accurate principle underlying its expression.

Freedom is the finest of the finer forces of nature, being essential to them all as it is co-operative and interpenetrative with truth.

Therefore men do not come into truth consciousness on any plane until they are free on that plane, because bondage on any plane limits the action thereon.

All intelligent action is free.

Freedom is entirely constructive. Any action which ignores the supreme law of goodness is ignorance, and there is no suggestion of freedom on any plane of thought and action which ignores the law.

All of the apparent evils of the earth planet are the result of expressed ignorance.

Men have lived in the thought that a perversion of truth means freedom, not realizing that any defiance of truth places them in most appalling bondage.

Even now, when the race is developing some degree of intelligence, human beings seem to imagine that lawlessness and licentiousness and a desecration of holy things mean freedom and that they are expressing freedom by ignoring duties which they have claimed and assumed as their own.

The human race is yet in its infant consciousness; it creates its own delusion, and as the babe plays with its toys and centers its interest on its dolls and tin soldiers, so does the human creature play with its conventions and its fashions and centers its interest in its troubles and its misunderstandings and enjoys its poor health, until it winds itself up in a web of bondage and perishes trying to get out of the bondage it has created.

And the human creature hugs itself and holds on tight to its own delusion; it loves its own limitation and it likes to play on its own wee sand pile, conceiving no greater freedom than to riotously romp thereon and to throw sand on those who are not quite so near to the top of the pile as they.

Every man has the attributes of freedom; he can think and he can act, he can love and he can learn, he can sow and he can reap, he can direct his own life action, and what Paul says or what the king does has nothing whatever to do with you or with me.

But we do not always know that we can think and we can do as seems wise to ourselves. We have been in thraldom so long that we have almost disintegrated in the dark of our dungeon of fear in our dread of somebody's or perhaps of many people's judgment.

The free man is conscious; he is awake to the divine word.

The bondman is unconscious; he environs himself with fear, and the word of truth does not penetrate his understanding.

One spark of God consciousness is more vitally important for human development and does more to uplift the race than barrels of bromidic platitudes and volumes of mentalized memories and indefinite plagiarism.

The earth planet has reached a plane be-

yond mere reason; it is entering the realm
of consciousness.

When the race is freed from any form of
limitation, the earth enters upon a higher or
more rapid era of its evolution, because the
intelligent earth responds to the finest thought
energy of its children.

And it is necessary that the earth be freed
from every bondage which holds it before it
can express at a more vitalized point; therefore when it is time for a great upliftment of
humanity, there is always the sweeping off
the earth those conditions and those people
who would hold it in the darkness and the
delusion of slavery.

Just as we see to-day, the earth must be
freed from monarchism and militarism before
it can enter into a new dimension of consciousness, and it will grovel in blood and woe
until the race frees itself from the dreadful
injustice which gives one man or a few men
control of millions, perhaps more worthy of
their brothers.

The earth planet and each and every one

of the suns and planets in the universe is intelligent and co-operative with the whole.

Every externalized atom is a form of expressed intelligent life, each one working from his angle for the God manifestation of the universe.

So long as the atom works from its angle in freedom, so long does it work in construction and in love and co-operative with the whole; when it is related to that which binds and destroys and compels in other directions than that which belongs to its intentive desire, it then does not do its perfect work.

Each atom works with every other atom for the good of the whole; freedom does not mean separation. The natural law of selection and its accompanying process of refining is the law of progress, just as human beings always succeed when they work with clean hands and a pure heart, which means an accurate motive in and for the thing they love.

Human beings are the only creatures which personalize God and defy the mighty forces of His universe, and while they get well

thrashed for so doing and accumulate about
them and in them all the destructive conditions which bind them to sorrow, they still
persist in their insane practises against the
finer forces of nature and then wonder at the
chaos of disease and death which rages around
them.

And, as the earth whirls on toward its finer
and freer consciousness, its children must
respond to its vibration and recall themselves
and become free to vibrate in the new earth
key by realizing the God of themselves, that
they may co-operate with the marvelous forces
which are now enfolding the earth and bringing it into the freer form of truth, where all is
life and there is no destruction.

Freedom always operates in order.

There can be nothing disorderly or confused
or riotous in freedom; it is equalized and
polarized, balanced and adjusted, in accurate
mathematical lines. And there is where humanity has erred in its conception of freedom;
as a race we have accepted the idea of it as
being something apart from order and of being

sort of an emotional quality, inaccurate and untrained, not realizing that any lack of balance leads to destruction and eventually to disintegration, while freedom itself is a part of life itself.

Freedom is of the universe an unlimited quality, although it is so often a hindered quality as to make it seem otherwise.

Freedom is the basis of operation of all forces, as every one of the finer forces must balance in freedom or it becomes perverted.

To illustrate — take the force of faith. When it is limited and bound it becomes fear, and its action is destructive. To do its perfect work faith must be unreserved and free.

We can also illustrate with the force of love. How wonderful is its free constructive action and how horrible when, in its bound and perverted state, it manifests as jealousy and hate!

· · ·

Every universal quality is manifested in the human being in the degree of his desire and his capacity, because man is the epitome of the universe and in him is the germ of every force which is expressed in the universe; to be sure, much of it is latent and all of it is crude, but in some degree is every atom of the man vibrating in its corresponding universal key.

Therefore, freedom is a human as well as a divine principle, and if the man would be accurate in his externalization and consequently true to himself and to all that concerns him, he will think free and so be free.

Freedom of human expression means that the body must respond to the soul demand through the medium of the mind; in other words, that the body, mind, and soul must vibrate in harmony, and as the human creature is making his present home upon the earth planet for the purpose of his soul experience and development, it is the natural and therefore the accurate and free thing for the soul demand to be the ruler of the man and of his earth life.

When the mind consciously ignores the soul demand and compels the repression of the body, sacrifice of the flesh always follows.

When the mind represses itself, thereby refusing to increase its capacity and power, sacrifice of far greater importance occurs, because
then the whole man is placed at a disadvan-
tage; he wastes his opportunity and weakens
his magnetism and places himself in the line
of limitation on every plane.

The soul never makes impossible demands;
it knows its own necessity, and when the man
is ready to respond to that necessity he soon
becomes free in body and in environment.

How often do you hear people say, "I
wanted to do thus and so, but was afraid I
could not afford it," or "afraid it might make
talk or somebody might object," and so they
deny the soul demand and crush out their
inspiration by repressing the desire which
would have led them into their next conscious step.

When we are true to our highest convic-
tion, true to truth, as it were, there is never
any question of what we can afford; we can
afford anything we need, and there is never
any question of what "they" may say; those

who are worthy of our consideration never criticize or condemn and those who do pass judgment upon us are simply infants in consciousness whose opinions are not sufficiently focused to influence us one way or another.

Understand, we are not speaking of sense or of sensual demands — those are of the flesh and will be balanced by the mind; we are speaking of the soul desire of the human being who is seeking to know himself and through that knowledge of himself, to know God.

The man who knows God is always free. Though his body may be locked in the deepest dungeon, he knows it is nothing in the light of a great awakening and he also knows that the locks and bars will dissolve when he is ready to be released.

The first attainment of the awakening human creature is to know how to discriminate between his soul desire and his sense demand.

The soul demand is always constructive and always relates to orderly adjustment.

The flesh desire is not always constructive,

because it is frequently expressed in ignorance and becomes riotous and causes mental
and physical confusion which is never possible
when the man permits himself to follow the
guidance of his soul.

The senses must be balanced and developed;
in the service of truth they are a mighty power
for good; when they are slaves to delusion and
to habit they are instruments of destruction,
and one of the most confusing of limitations is
that which results from allowing the senses
to dominate the mind.

It is sense domination and mind subjuga-
tion thereof which prevents the man from
following the desire of his soul, and the result
is that the flesh shrivels and the brains of the
flesh, which should be perfect instruments of
the mind, become atrophied and then the
whole structure becomes a crumbling monu-
ment to falsity instead of a glorifying temple
of truth.

Freedom is essentially a subtle permeating
activity; it is sensitive and dependent upon
harmony and truth.

You cannot compel freedom any more than you can compel love, because under compulsion it loses its quality and ceases to be freedom, just as under any compelling thought love loses its constructive power and turns into aversion and fear which soon manifests in hate.

Freedom must express from the within out; the man who is free in mind soon becomes free in body, and then he becomes free in expression, because his recognition of his soul requirements leads him into those experiences which he requires in the earth phase of his life lessons.

One of the vitally important lessons which we must learn in our attainment of freedom is, that if we would be free ourselves we must leave every other soul in absolute freedom so far as we are concerned; we may help him, we may inspire him, provided, of course, it is his desire that we should; otherwise we must have no judgment of any sort concerning him.

When a person arrives at the age of responsibility, which means when he has the ability

to respond to the demands of his own life
requirements, he will know that he is the cause
of those requirements and in his own way he
must assume them and fulfil them; he should
not be handicapped by opinion or bound by
other people's desires — and if you and I interfere with him and attempt to force him into
our way of seeing and doing, he is more than
liable to fail and his failure will react upon us
and place us in some sort of bondage to him.

Most of human trouble and confusion — in
fact, we might say, all of its pain — results from
the bondage in which men hold each other.
They do not know that one human being
cannot possibly own another and that if they
hold another in slavery or permit themselves
to be held there, it always reacts on all parties
concerned and causes untold misery on every
plane.

Each form of nature's manifestation, as
well as each human being, evolves according
to its capacity, and it should be free to express
its life in the degree of its development.

The dog has his conception of freedom; he

is not bound by moral law or financial griev-
ance, but he demands a master and claims his
divine right of service to that master.

The child changes its form of limitation
step by step, and as it advances into its larger
life it assumes many phases of bondage which
must be necessary in its development or it
would not attract them and attach them to
itself.

Many times we attract a greater bondage in
our effort to escape something which we have
assumed and from which we imagine we are
freeing ourselves, and quite frequently we make
such a strenuous race after happiness that we
become abject slaves and make ourselves really
miserable in the seeking.

Freedom, like every other of nature's finer
forces and activities, can be very closely imi-
tated, and the real thing is often quite obscured
by its outside appearance.

The true human manifestation of freedom
is freedom of consciousness.

In consciousness is the truth realization
which is absolutely chaste; it knows no evil,

passes no opinion or judgment, and sees humanity as the expression of God.

He who is free in consciousness is free indeed, for he is related to the opulence of the universe, to the truth of life, and to the goodness of his own being.

He who is bound in his consciousness may be lord of all he surveys and still be an abject slave to habit or to some delusion of his own creation.

When truth is free to express itself in man, all things are added, and nothing of good can possibly be withheld from him who is free in his conscious realization of God.

Verily, when all men become free in their consciousness and conscious in their freedom, every appearance of evil shall vanish from the face of the earth, and there shall be no more sorrow and no more tears, for truth shall rise supreme and claim its own.

STUDY CONCERNING HEALING

When you pray, let your prayer be for the glory and the uplifment of the things that are.

Pray that the cabbage sprout may become a glorious cabbage, rather than that it may turn into a rose.

Pray that the law be divinely fulfilled, rather than that you may defeat the law.

And always, and always, pray so constructively that the soul shine of you is omnipresent in your life.

EALING is the process of reconstructing that which has attracted
destruction.

The healing process replaces what is ap-
parently lost, balances the forces which are
out of the truth line, and recalls to consciousness the child of good who has left his father's
home to slumber in the wilderness.

The human race is in the throes of dissolution, and it must be healed; it must repent
and recall, and readjust itself unless it would
disintegrate and dissolve as though it never
was.

The process of disintegration is painful
and the race suffers.

Suffering is not a force nor yet a substance;
it is the result of a grievous lack of something
on some plane of conscious expression, and
pain is the warning of that lack or, in other
words, a result of the lack, just as happiness

is the result of completeness and not a definite force externalized.

Health, as we comprehend it, is the balanced and complete expression of the flesh body.

Health, in reality, is the balanced and complete expression of every phase and of every form of life manifestation.

Healing is not only a process of reconstructing the body, but for reconstructing confused conditions in the individual life externalization.

Healing means regeneration on all planes.

When human beings, through lack of health degenerate on any plane, it is because they have misdirected their portion of the universal life energy and thereby thrown themselves out of balance with its co-operative action; as it is expressed in the parable of the prodigal son — out of their Father's house.

When the lack is lack of love, it is especially disastrous, because love is the cohesive force of the universe and absence of love means a weakening of every one of nature's finer forces; such a weakening causes degeneracy of all points, which, naturally, leads to acute poverty of flesh and of purse.

However, if the man has so placed himself in the wilderness, where he dwells with the swine of disease and poverty and sin, his condition is far from hopeless, because he can always recall and repent and return to the mighty and glorious intelligence of the universe, which is, in truth, His home and where the loving Father always welcomes straying prodigal children to his abundant and complete storehouse, which is abundantly filled with health and wealth and wisdom and love.

The human race has reached the point in its evolution where it is aware that the process of dissolution is rising rampant within its most vitalized center and that its only salvation depends upon its recalling itself and returning to truth, which is the balanced action of the universe and therefore the evidence of God.

Most forcibly does the race realize that it has forgotten its divinity and its angelhood and turned to brutality and is cultivating its swine consciousness until its God-ness is over-shadowed and disease claims mastery of the flesh and of the whole life externalization.

The opportunity to throw off this disease is now — because the human desire for emancipation from poverty is aroused; verily, the children of the earth home are rising to consciousness and demanding their birthright of their Father's home.

. .

Healing is a natural constructive process.

There is no limit to the power of any constructive current, but its operation may be restricted by being deflected from its intentioned course by some destructive or intrusive thought form which emanates from environing minds or from some disturbing external condition.

Healing is a living, enduring force which operates in the atmosphere of wisdom and love.

The healing current is absolute and accurate and all-powerful when you are true to yourself and constructive in your attitude to life — it never fails when both patient and healer agree to co-operate with the divine consciousness of perfect being.

If you are reaching out into the infinite and healing yourself, you will co-operate with yourself by harmonizing your body and your mind and your soul, thereby bringing yourself into the divine consciousness of perfect being.

Truth is the accurate action of that divine consciousness, and therefore admits of no compromise.

The healing current must operate in truth, and there is no halfway process in truth; it demands all, even as it gives all, and in the pure, chaste atmosphere of truth, no unclean thing can possibly exist, because the truth atmosphere dissolves all inharmony and all disease, no matter on what plane it may be expressed.

The finer forces of the universe are not regulated by manual effort, but by mental mastery.

The physical body of man is the concentrated magnet for all the forces of nature, and it is also the instrument and the transmitter for the intelligent regulation of the universal thought force.

The desire energy is the first response to human thought activity; as the desire qualifies and discriminates in point of selection, so the will energizes and promotes the action of desire and completes the work of formulating whatever force of nature has been selected by the man through the motive energy of his desire.

The will is a soul force; it acts immediately upon the intelligence of the flesh atoms and especially upon those atoms which control most directly the thought energy.

Therefore the will, in the form of the intentive force, controls the emotions and is the primal factor to be considered in the study of the healing process which must first be related to the polarization of emotion.

The natural condition of the human being is one of freedom.

Freedom always means co-operation with the law of all expressed life; it relates to health of every plane of being, and health is the natural, orderly, constructive, equalized distribution of all the forces of life.

Lack of health is a condition of bondage.

It is a result of misdirected energy and is an unnatural, disorderly, destructive plane of being.

Lack of health is a condition of negative disorder which cannot possibly be recognized by an infinite consciousness, because in the universal or cosmic completeness nothing unnatural can possibly exist.

The man himself is the cause as he is the continuance of all his diseases and inharmonies; all ills of the flesh and all lack of supply are caused and nourished and entirely governed by his disorderly mental action.

Many of the earth children allow themselves to live in the delusive thought that afflictions are the result of the will of God; not realizing that if God is the promoter of affliction and death, men have not the power, even if they have the desire, to overcome that supreme will — and that it is blasphemous for them to make the attempt to thus defy so omnipotent and autocratic a ruler.

But, glory be to the light of infinite Truth and Love, to-day we know that the God of our love is worthy of our absorbing devotion; we know that He is the heart of our heart and the life of our life and that in His great love consciousness there is no recognition of abnormality and therefore we know that in Truth there is no disease and its accompanying despair.

And there is always the glorious nature supply which in all its abundance enfolds the divine human creature, even though he may have separated himself from the supernal law of being which declares that all is God, and even though he has shut out the light and entered into the realm of nothingness, he still has the privilege of re-entering his Father's home, the truth realm, and of becoming the free creature which the natural law demands; free and natural and opulently endowed.

When a man finds himself in darkness, in the bondage of sickness and poverty and sin,

his first move toward reconstruction is to
recognize his desire in the matter of selection
and then to decide exactly what he wants.
Shall he select the truth realm of ease or shall
he choose the delusion realm of disease?

If he declares for delusion, it is his privilege to abide therein until his soul lays down
its human temple because of the destructive
force which he attracts.

If he declares for truth and its attributes of
Health and Wealth and Opulence and Love,
let him change the polarity of his structure
by deciding that he will be related to the health
life and that no forces but those that are constructive shall ever again contract him.

Having decreed that he will attach himself
to constructive life, let him turn his attention to the restoring forces of nature and intelligently relate himself to them until he
can utilize his intention and his energy consciously in reorganizing his flesh and in regen-
erating his entire being.

As human life on the earth goes on, the in-
stinct of the individual expression of that life

should grow stronger day by day; men should continually demand a more vital manifestation of beauty and strength and happiness instead of becoming, as they frequently do, quite reconciled to the idea of being inactive and unbeautiful, a burden to themselves and an object of toleration to their fellow-men.

There is a motive cause for every differentiation of energy; if men grow inactive or unbeautiful when they have lived beyond the first few years of youth, they alone are the cause, as they alone reflect the result, and the pity of it is that it is all a lack of understanding of their relation to life, which always means an unbalancing of forces.

In natural youth, the constructive forces act with more rapidity than the destructive. The result is constant and rapid up-building which we call growth.

In youth we have more love and less wisdom; as we accumulate experiences which may deflect our love, we gain more wisdom, and love is less in evidence — in youth it is love without wisdom and in age it is wisdom without love.

The cultivation of wisdom apart from its necessary comrade, love, causes the destructive forces to act with more rapidity than the constructive, and the result is inevitably disintegration.

If we would have health, if we would remain a long time on the earth home, if we would be healthy on all planes, which means happy, while we are here, we will learn to balance our love and our wisdom so that they become construction itself. Then we eliminate with our wisdom whatever does not nourish the flesh and whatever destroys our life harmony and we attract with our love the form of life energy and the substance of the earth which harmonizes with us and which contains the life essences which are essential to our upbuilding.

That form of energy which is applied to the work of restoration and regeneration we call the healing force, and while it is very little understood by the occidental students of to-day, they recognize it as a constructive activity which is a factual element in modern manifestation, and it is true that any recognition of constructive power is the first step toward reconstructive understanding and eventual accomplishment.

Healing of the flesh by mental energy has been practised by the students of occult law ever since the beginning of the earth's history; in every age and generation different systems have been exploited by the different prophets of the time.

Many of the oriental healers relate the man to the solar system; they are students of astrology and students of human anatomy, and every bone atom and every flesh atom and nerve atom has its place in their realization of the correspondence of the man to the Zodiac. Then with constructive and intelligent system they adjust the patient to his normal position in the universe and balance him with his place therein.

The constructive thinker is he who is the healer, whatever system he may use; any alive force will overbalance a negative one, and the man who lives because he loves to live and who sees joy in his daily work is doing the healing and the saving work for himself and for every one around him, because his intention is always good.

The soul who is unafraid is another savior of his fellow-men; he makes the way plain for the beautiful faith energy which is the spirit of healing and of accomplishment.

It is the cold, clammy nothingness of fear which holds mankind in bondage and which numbs the will and chills the heart and induces impotency.

There is no place in human expression for the thing we call fear unless we intend to destroy the flesh because it is the direct antithesis of faith and is as degenerative to the flesh atoms as faith is regenerative to them.

Faith intensifies the will and increases its activity on every line; in essence it is constructive, it unites the individual intention with the universal will.

Hope is a force of illuminative quality; it lightens the path and makes possible the operation of faith.

Hope follows desire and precedes every other of the finer forces of nature.

Hope is strengthened by the power of imaging, which is of the greatest value in every sort of attainment.

. . .

Hope always images good; it has no place outside of the constructive vision, and so it restores the spiritual balance and dissolves despair.

If we would reconstruct ourselves and re-relate ourselves to God, we will know that these finer forces of nature are practical forces of life which we can use in our mental operation. We will know there are no miracles, there never have been any miracles; all these things which we do not quite understand are merely the natural operation of the law, but we have not yet reached the place of the finer comprehension.

Jesus the Christ told us concerning these

finer forces of nature; He explained our universal relationship and illustrated it in what are called miracles. But many of the things he told were suppressed, and much of what was told was distorted, until the race has misinterpreted His teaching as it has misinterpreted Him and many who walked before Him.

It is the time; the race and the earth planet itself are demanding to be healed, to be balanced and adjusted to God's life.

Love must be liberated, Truth must be revealed, the old delusions must pass away, and men must walk with God if they would hold their place in The Father's home.

> A slumbering world awakes
> And quivering with the fire of truth
> Declares its freedom.
>
> Mankind decrees its own;
> It shall dissolve its crushing woe
> In love of good.

Sin shall not be;
Its attributes of anguish shall dissolve
In God's pure word.

For God alone
In this most glorious coming day,
Shall reign supreme.

STUDY CONCERNING THE FOURTH DIMENSION

I look out over the earth home
And a marvelous thing is there;
  A quivering, living awaking,
  A wonderful day abreaking
On sea and earth and in air.

Behold the atoms of earth life,
Anew and aglow and aflame;
  With something sweet interblending,
  With consciousness all extending,
And nothing quite the same.

And within my soul responding
Comes the answer to years of prayer,
  'Tis the human child awaking,
  His heart to God is abreaking
In His holy truth aware.

Behold the glory of earth life
As the wisdom of God we proclaim;
  The real of us beams transcendent;
  Our day is dawning transplendent
For our love is aglow and aflame.

Study Concerning the Fourth Dimension

A DIMENSION is an accurate measurement of the race consciousness in its adjustment to its part of the universal life externalization.

Out of the unmanifest, life is becoming manifest, and it manifests and externalizes according to the thought activity of the universe.

Any manifestation of form or condition in any realm or on any planet in the universe is the result of the co-operative race thought of the thinkers on that planet.

Evolution depends upon thought, thought depends upon the thinkers, and as they become more and more conscious of their relationship to the universe, their thought becomes more rapid and they measure themselves and their portion of life in a finer and more powerful key.

We are externalizing our part of life upon the earth planet, our angle of vision is from the earth, and so we will study this subject of dimensions from the earth angle.

We use the term "dimension" to define a distinct point of differentiation in the race evolution — a definite advance in race consciousness through human mental measurement.

The race advances as a unit — when enough souls are ready for a step in consciousness, the great realization becomes factualized and evident in all life manifestation; it is as a new world opening to humanity wherein they are willing to cast aside their former limitations and become free in their newer relation to God and His earth home and more attuned with His intentive goodness.

He who concentrates his portion of the infinite mind in relating himself to all the good of the unmanifest is co-operating with the infinite intelligence in causing the good manifestation.

The human creature is the epitome of the

universe; he is part of it and united with it;
he is interpenetrated with it and all of its
experiences; therefore the human measurement influences the universe as the universal
measurement influences humanity.

Life is externalized on the earth planet in
the degree of the desire angle of the earth
occupants.

Human life is externalized according the
the desire quality of the individual; as he
thinks in his heart, he becomes in his life
expression, and he takes his place upon the
earth at exactly the point where he has placed
himself in his estimate of himself.

If I have measured myself so that I am only
conscious of my physical sense requirement,
my body will only use its physical sense intelligence and my life forces will vibrate to my
physical sense demand; therein I have limited
myself to a dimension which has not evolved
beyond the physical sense consciousness.

It is quite possible in such a case that by
refusing to relate myself to finer and freer
understanding and not being willing to vi-

brate with a broader humanity that I may
by my limitation attract poverty of body or
mind into my atmosphere and so interfere
with the race progress.

And such interference means that I must
change my relationship and go with my race
or I must leave my present abode and go to
some realm in the universe in which I shall
find my place.

When the individual feels the urge of his
soul for a freer relationship and a broader
life expression, he must measure himself to
it; when he is ready to enter that plane he
will forget his former limitation and commence anew to further the progress of himself
and of his race.

When the individual becomes interested in
the study of dimensions, his consciousness is
already merging into another dimension, and
his consciousness does not require profound
mathematical calculation to prove the truth
concerning it; his is the child heart which
comprehends it.

Many things which are intricate and difficult to the highly trained materialist are as clear as sunlight to the spiritually attuned mind, because all things are simplified through love and the Cosmic or spiritual thinker thinks in his heart brain in love.

· ·

Jesus Christ was the prophet who ushered in the first rays of consciousness which relate to the Fourth Dimension; in Him was the trinity merged into the cross or the square and humanity more unified with Divinity.

In Jesus Christ the saving of His race was solving the problem of death, which is to be merged into life in the on-coming dimension when the last enemy shall be overcome.

Death, which is the last enemy, shall be overcome when men know the truth concerning the resurrection and the life and it is a fact that we, as a race, are coming more clearly into the knowledge of life and its eternal opportunity every day.

Material science takes one part or one fact and visualizes the whole from that fact, while spiritual science takes the whole and perceives the one fact and all of the individual facts from knowledge of the whole; one is working from the finite toward the infinite, and the other is recognizing the infinite and consequently knowing the finite.

We know very little by mere physical sense consciousness; we cannot by physical perception realize the existence of the soul, and if our vision is purely material we are likely to say there is no such thing as our own soul, for we cannot make real our own selves except by realizing God in our selves. But we can, through super-consciousness or spiritual consciousness which is the divine realization, realize the soul and its forces and attributes; we can therein and thereby make real our own selves, and so we can comprehend in the degree of our desire the God intention and our part of its activity.

The light of the next Dimension is the illumination of the souls of men; in its light we shall move beyond the limitations of human opinion and we shall unfold ourselves out of opinion into reality; we shall realize our true

selves as apart from delusion and aware of
our divinely human nature.

Each dimension of universal consciousness
is composed of a vast variety of differing
degrees of involving and evolving states of
consciousness, resulting from our life experiences, and whether we select our experiences
on this earth planet or elsewhere, they are
exactly what we require for the particular
phase of expression toward which our desire
is leading us.

The children of the earth home are supposed
to be in the third dimension of universal consciousness; in other words, we are living in a
world of three dimensions, which means that
we are mentally measuring ourselves in the
third angle of our human capacity — but
the race is strengthening its capacity, and
when the earth people become so vitalized in
their present earth dimension that it over-
balances its present measurement, they will
then extend the acute angle of the third dimension and measure themselves in the right
angle of the fourth.

A third dimension implies a second, and a second dimension implies a first, and one and all are merging or interrelating one with the other; naturally the greater force is conscious of the lesser, while the lesser does not realize the greater until it develops to the same strength of the greater and so becomes conscious of it and equal to expression on its plane.

So from our plane of consciousness in the third dimension, we may easily perceive the sphere or the quality or the strength of the first and of the second, but until we evolve to the plane of the fourth dimension, we cannot possibly realize its realm of action, although we may contemplate it, and by thinking concerning it with a constructive desire we will inevitably relate ourselves to it.

As we think and study and meditate upon this next realm of our life manifestation, we become more and more attuned to its atmosphere and we commence to perceive its freedom and its quality of vibratory force and thereby we draw its thought waves into our own atmosphere so that we bring its wonderful quality of interpenetration upon ourselves until we become a part of its broader expression and so have the privilege and the opportunity of helping our entire race to approach its finer freedom.

. .

All schools of philosophy have some theory concerning the measure of life; most of them are so complicated that the theory remains only theory — but there is one sweet and simple sect who are sometimes called spiritualists, who have an explanation of dimensions and their form of mental measurement in such easy language that any lover of truth, whatever his creed or however strong his prejudice, can easily understand.

According to their philosophy, the first dimension is length, wherein the human physical sense perceives only the strength line of forward and back and the individual mind measures its part of life in a direct line, with no variation and no swerving from the path of its selection, no side glance or uplift, with

only the finer force of hope, which pertains
to the first dimension, perceiving and relating
it to future dimensions.

Hope connects with its own quality of
intention, which belongs to the second
dimension, so the thread of the intentive consciousness connects with hope and enters the
straight and direct line of the first dimension — and with the union of hope and intention, the human sense perceives a curve and
with it comes a realization of breadth, and the
mind action swerves into the circular motion
of the second dimension, replacing the straight
line of the first, or rather uniting the two.

The race then measures itself in the two
dimensions of length and breadth, thereby
enlarging its life manifestation and making
it possible to connect with the third.

Hope and Intention in unison with expectation finally vivify the mind of the human
creature until the race enters the third measurement of its consciousness (thickness) in
the trinity of its human dimension, where it is
rapidly merging into a broader or a higher

measurement which will give it a fourth dimension of consciousness with an added and far greater power which will relate it to increasing strength and therefore lead it into many more dimensions of transcendental scope.

In our present limited mental measurement we are so closely related to the quality of fear that we have not yet dared to really concentrate our forces upon a different dimension than we now understand; it is only the few who are unafraid and only the few who know that Fear has no place in the right angle of human expression.

Language belongs to the second and third dimensions, so it is difficult to explain in words things that are beyond words, and much of the thought concerning the fourth dimension must be given through suggestion and through thought transference, which belongs to its measurement.

While we may not be required to explain these things which appear to be beyond explanation, as we each come into the finer glimpse and the freer experiences which lead us to a broader measurement of ourselves, we may through our suggestions help others out of the narrower path, from hope into realization of the finer accuracy of our portion of the infinite manifestation.

There is never any favor shown by an infinite intelligence. The individual who perceives a finer force does so because he has the quality of the finer force within himself.

No man has the gift of seeing or hearing or knowing more than another — Justice is a perfect form of love and God is just as He is wise and loving, and when we are ready, our portion of His life enlarges to meet our readiness.

Emanuel Swedenborg, who is one of the great prophets, gives us the idea of the measurement of consciousness through and by the law of motion, sometimes called vibration, thus: 1st, Straight; 2d, Circular; 3d, Spiral; 4th, Vortexian.

Here are a few suggestions from other seers which from their viewpoint express the four differing measurements of human consciousness.

1st,—	2nd,—	3rd,—	4th,—
Length.	Breadth.	Thickness.	Throughness.
Straight.	Circular.	Spiral.	Vortexian.
Hope.	Intention.	Expectation.	Realization
Love.	Wisdom.	Construction.	Fulfilment.
Faith.	Understanding.	Work.	Accomplishment.
Body.	Mind.	Soul.	Ego.

One might go on indefinitely concerning the merging of nature's finer forces from one form of expression into another, in other words, from their present dimension into the next or from the third dimension into the fourth — except that here again we may err because the next dimension is merely our measurement of the force which, through our broader realization, enlarges our consciousness.

The next dimension and many beyond dimensions are here now, always have been, and always will be, although the human creature fails to perceive more than his capacity permits — and, alas, he limits his capacity by his own selfish and introspective measurement of himself.

. .

Have you ever felt that your vision of life was transcending your present measurement of your part of life? There comes over you sort of a prophetic thrill which might be memory and it might be prophecy, you scarcely know except that it is some kind of a fleeting thought formulation which seems to be beyond your present capacity to solidify — you cannot quite tell and you cannot hold on to it; of course, you do not yet know, but might it not be your glimpse of another dimension, a consciousness of things not definitely manifest although already a subconscious part of your life?

Again, have you sometimes known that a presence unseen, yet vitally real, was with you, almost a part of you — and have you perceived a wonderful transcendent realm interpenetrating your commonplace, everyday environment? Possibly you have heard a strain of music or a breath of fresh sweet odor has swept over you, seeming to connect you with another realm. Might it not be a glimpse of finer, different forces faintly relating you to another measurement of your own part of life which you are recognizing a trifle more clearly every day?

If we would only think on these things, welcome them into our part of life, and accept the fact that we do not yet know everything there is to know, instead of casting them aside as unworthy of our common sense, we would be showing a much finer common sense as well as relating ourselves to the opulent current of a distinctly opulent life wave; too often it is our own prejudice and our own contempt that holds us in the bondage of poverty on all planes.

Out of the dim dark nothingness
There comes a glorified sight,
As though the gray murky mistiness
Merges in clear living light.

The recognition of a force or of a condition gives us a certain relationship to it, and if we qualify with it, we will eventually solidify it with our own part of life. To illustrate: If we recognize the forces of construction, such as love and faith and kindness, etc., and practically practise them and so relate ourselves to them, we bring the constructive quality into our life manifestation in such solidified expression that it permeates us and our atmosphere, and all that we do and all that we possess vibrate in the key of success.

On the contrary, if we recognize any forces of destruction, such as jealousy or resentment or condemnation, etc., to the extent of entertaining them in our minds, we will permeate our bodies with disease and our financial and home conditions will be unhappy and unsuccessful and we may really think and so declare that we are unlucky and the victims of fate.

It is an easy matter to blame some one else for our misfortune and to give ourselves credit for our good fortune when we know in our heart of hearts that we are the cause, as we are the effect, of our own intentive desire.

All of these various forms of destructive force which are disintegrating the children of men, will be dissolved when mankind refuses to recognize the forces of destruction which express themselves in the forms of life activity which we call evil; when men entertain only good in their minds, then only good can exist in their flesh and in their lives and evil cannot BE; naturally disease and poverty and other formulations of the thing formerly known as evil must also disappear.

It is only through and by the recognition of good, and good means the expression of God's life, that the race can measure itself in the right angle of truth and so enter into the consciousness of another dimension.

· ·

Existence in matter requires form, and expression in form requires magnetic and intentive and operative ability of an infinite intelligence.

In his present measurement of himself, the human creature does not realize that he is part of this infinite intelligence and that his responsibility is with and for the universal manifestation of the universal spirit substance.

Mankind must evolve itself unto God —

in other words, man must make good the
thing which he has assumed and that is his
own part of God's life.

Every man has the ability to respond to
the desire of his soul, and his responsibility
cannot and does not extend beyond his highest
claim for himself.

The finer the spiritual perception of the
man, the more magnetic and able becomes his
power of attracting the idea and of anchoring
it in form.

We sometimes term a fine human perception of spirit force and the accurate conception of expressing it, as art — and it is true
that the artist is the prophet and the lover of
his dimension.

He may express his art in oratory or states-
manship, he may prefer to reveal it with his
brush or his pen or his chisel or his violin,
he may be a clerk or a cook, a business man
or a home maker, whatever his taste in his
work, he is an artist when he expresses the
divine of him in that work because he measures himself by his love for it, and whether

its manifestation is taking the cubist form of the fourth dimension in its sound or speech or color or form, or whether it takes the form of a second or a third measurement, it is divine because it expresses the highest and holiest desire of the man.

It is the human perception of the finer forces of nature which links the finite with the infinite, and it is the increasing human faith and understanding which is blending the human with the divine, interpenetrating matter with spirit, thereby spiritualizing the whole and so accomplishing the perfect work of atonement or of at-one-ment in the all God.

The reason we are so dense in our comprehension of our own opportunity and ability and of our own futurity, is that we are so filled with our own self-love that we have no place within us for the love of God.

Most people are so immersed in the desires of their flesh bodies that they almost destroy the body by centering a too dynamic thought force upon it; we should be far stronger on every plane, healthier and richer and more intelligent, if we would think out toward our fellow-man rather than in toward ourselves, because then we could permit the God life to enter into our innermost being and consequently we should be interpenetrated with the all good.

Service to humanity means relationship with divinity, oneness with the Father, and in that relationship, all things are added and the fullness of infinite blessing becomes centered in the human child who serves because he loves and who loves because he serves.

There is no place apart from God, and soon His humanity shall be aware of His omnipresence, for the hour of a new measurement of human consciousness is upon the earth home.

That which has seemed mysterious is fast losing its mystery, and it will be well for the race if it use its interpenetrative knowledge and power for good and for the upliftment and the advancement of the entire race.

It is not so long ago that men were startled

with the idea that they could actually speak to each other across the miles through the medium of a wire; to-day I read of the wireless telephone, an instrument so attuned that the voice is carried without the wire.

How long do you suppose it will be before the message will be carried with neither wire nor instrument — by attuning the ear to hear the soundless sound? Only until the man is willing to know his own power of mind and heart and brain, only until his desire to know the truth of himself and of his part of life is greater than outside delusion.

The few have always known, but only the few are unafraid.

Soon all humanity must know that the lifting of the veil shall be, that veil of unconsciousness which is already ragged and weak from the onslaughts of knowledge which have been especially rapid during these later years of the third dimension.

The soul desire of the man is the force which leads him to the broader and more accurate measurement of himself — and it is the intentive force within which, following hope and merging into expectation, relates him to the accomplished fulfilment of his desire and he realizes that he is aware of a fourth dimension of consciousness wherein he measures his life and its conditions without fear and with interpenetrative good on all planes of his manifestation of that life.

The important thing is that men shall desire to know of greater things than they have yet realized — let them open their minds and their hearts to hear the response to their desires, for the spirit of truth and of love which permeates all space and inspires all life never fails to respond to the desire for knowledge, although the fear of the man sometimes obscures the answer to his prayer.

There is nothing marvelous or mysterious in the search for knowledge concerning the viewless path; in the early days of its first visioning, it was supposed to be a path of pain or despair, because the first faint glimpse was one of mystery and consequently of fear.

But the mystery has vanished and the fear is no more — the path is before us in clear, beautiful, and flower-banked view. The God of the all life reveals Himself as good, He claims mankind as His children, and it rests with His children whether or not they shall abide in and with Him.

There is no lack in God's great life, for He is good.

There is no fear in God's great heart, for He is love.

There is no grief in God's dear home, for He knows all.

Mankind shall know of life and they shall breathe into their hearts His love and into their minds His wisdom.

There shall be no fear and no lack in the earth home, for the earth people shall recognize the mighty constructive intention of the ever living God.

His love shall be fulfilled in humanity and they shall sing the song of life and walk the path of another dimension in joy and gladness.

A wonderful day is adawning,
The glorious hour is come
When the prayer of a race is answered
As a mighty task is finished
And a greater work is begun.

It is not my concern if you are harsh or unjust to me; it is only my affair that I am kind and just to you.

It is not for me to judge my neighbor, nor is it my place to dictate to him the line of his path; it is my part to regulate my own angle of action and to attend to keeping my own dooryard clean.

It is not of use to me or my fellow-man that I should recognize the thing called evil; it is only useful for me to know that God is good and to be so aware of Him and His goodness that I may become a light unto the path of all who pass my way.

For God is all and only in His living breath and in His loving heart can life and you and I eternally endure.

STUDY OF EXPERIENCE

What could I know of life
Had I not lived?

How could I tell
Of loss of earthly joy
And gain of God,
Of giving back to earth
The heavy clod which bound my soul
But that I KNOW?

So what of pain,
If through its open door
Come gifts more glorious
Than one has known before?

Aye, gifts of freer life
And grander love
Of God.

Study of Experience

XPERIENCE is the result of actual life happenings.

No man can learn living things for another any more than one man can measure or judge any other human creature. We may profit by our brother's experience as humanity evolves by the race experience, but our individual attainment comes through our own actual experience.

Because experience follows desire, our own quality of desire, and so results in the assimilation of these finer forces of nature to which we have practically and factually related ourselves through our individual desire and its response which is materialized in experience.

Every force in the universe is latent in the creature that is made in the image of God, because the universe is God, and whenever this divinely imaged man is ready and capable of externalizing these forces and using them, he relates himself to the realm which he requires,

so the developing soul selects the earth planet
for his home whenever he is ready for the earth
experience.

The whole Cosmos is a formulated breathing result of divine experience, and Truth
bears witness to the absolute good of the
holy involution and evolution of universal
experience.

Ofttimes the man is almost stranded by his
vanity and selfishness and so refuses the experience that he needs; also it sometimes
occurs that the man nearly obliterates himself by his fear and personal introspection and
cannot quite reach the place of his needed
experience.

Which is the reason we are taught that the
one essential thing in life is that men must
know themselves and not fall into utter dissolution by deceiving themselves.

It sometimes happens that we fail to assimilate or even to accept the lesson of our experience, and it is then that Mother Nature
accentuates the experience and compels our
attention in the form of pain, because if we re-

fuse to be responsible for that which we have attracted and assumed, the infinite law which is the intentive force of an infinite intelligence will show us the sure and certain way.

One of the limiting forces in our human reach toward the divine vision is regret; we demand experience, we call on life to unfold its mysteries to us, we feel ourselves inspired to draw to ourselves the living response to our craving souls, and then after our divine daring, we weaken and are afraid.

Verily it is not surprising that we lose our youth and our beauty, our health and our joy of living, when we thwart ourselves and our beautiful unfoldment with the paralyzing energy of regret.

Of what are we afraid? —

There is absolutely nothing to fear except our own delusion; there is no such thing as "They say." People are not nearly so interested in our affairs as we seem to think, and when we are true to ourselves, we very soon become true to everybody else, and then we find ourselves loving everybody, and when we really

love other people there is no question about
their loving us, and when people love us, they
love the things we do.

The soul claim is always for expanding and
enlarging life, that it may evolve and know
more of God and so become Godlike; and we
do not become Godlike through any separation
from God's creatures. Any philosophy which
teaches us separation from another human
creature or another phase of God's life is
the wrong brand of philosophy.

The only philosophy which experience proves
true is that God is and we, you and I, are
one with God.

.   .

Through experience, problems are solved,
great things are accomplished, humanity becomes finer and freer in the activities of life; it
may not always be a comfortable process, but it
surely is an alive one if there are to be results.

It may take a huge war, the actual smash-
ing of bodies, to bring men out of the torpor
of slavery, but who will deny that any experience which frees the human race from bondage

and relates it to the greatness and the equality of individuals is worth any price?

Can you imagine a bondman entering the kingdom of God where all men are equal.

It takes slaves to make tyrants, and it belongs to the slave to free himself.

When God's children refuse to be murderers, militarism will be no more.

When men refuse to worship the false gods of aristocracy and money power, monarchies will dissolve.

Surely the ages of experience which have held mankind in hell should now show them the way into the place where they may have the privilege of being true to themselves and helping to greaten the world instead of using their intelligence to destroy it.

Experience teaches us our relationship to and with each other, which is the most important part of our relationship with life.

We cannot realize or even understand a condition which is not within range of our experience, not that we must necessarily do the thing but that we are capable of doing it if we are capable of formulating it in our minds; therefore we do not condemn the action of our fellow-man unless we are capable of the same action, otherwise we could not understand it sufficiently to judge it, and usually the closer it is to our own line of action the more loudly we denounce it.

Likewise our appreciation of any glorious good and holy motive comes through our recognition of it and the fact that somewhere along the line of our expression, whether in the earth life or elsewhere, it has been part of our experience.

Experience is the most valuable possession in the world. We journey from world to world and from realm to realm for the purpose of accumulating experience and thereby coming into an understanding of life in all its varying forms and, unlike many of our possessions, we may use it and we do use it constantly, or give it away in unlimited quantities, and it increases in strength and power for all of time.

As possessions lead to expression, they

naturally add to themselves by the power of their own action — so we have the old occult teaching that "to him that hath, shall be given and to him that hath not, shall be taken away," because possessions, be they mental or moral or metallic, will add to themselves by the law of their own magnetic energy.

Therefore the man who invites experience finds himself plentifully endowed with many and various sorts of the thing he seeks, all increasing his power, and, if he is true to himself, each one adding to his soul energy and strength.

Experience gives the human creature his divinely human balance; it relates his love and his wisdom, it adjusts his faith and his understanding, it steadies his fanaticism and makes of him a holy man.

The fanatic has unlimited love — love for cause or he would not be a fanatic, love for people or he would not try to compel them to accept his cause, and love for God or he would not sacrifice himself for what he BELIEVES is absolute good — but the fanatic works without experience, and so he lacks the balancing force of wisdom, which is needed by love to give it creative and constructive power; so his creative power is void and he fails to externalize the thing he loves.

Each man's position in the universe is distinct and different from every other man's position; consequently each man's experience is distinct and different, and yet as each force is humanized by each individual experience, it adds to the strength and power of all humanity, and every force which is made practical in human expression is made manifest by human experience.

We live for experience and we live from experience. If we wish to develop our soul energy and increase our power, we do not sit in our own dooryard and luxuriate in its peace and repose; rather we assume our place in the turmoil of life and attract to ourselves as much experience as we can assimilate and utilize.

In reality there is never any end to anything which is true, because everything of truth is imperishable in essence; but the form of truth varies and experiences change, and atoms and men and worlds are constantly regenerated and reconstructed and remanifested in newer and more complete forms by the increasing activity of their experiences.

Every atom of spirit is reaching out for broader consciousness and greater power; when one phase of expression is completed or one form of experience is assimilated, another manifestation of life upon a higher spiral of evolution takes its place and a different and purer experience awaits our attention.

Experiences are as the stepping stones leading forward and onward, one dissolving into another and that one merging into others and all working toward grander and more complete consciousness of the soul.

Anyone who attempts to violate the law, whether physical, social, moral, or financial, invites destruction upon the plane of his attempted violation; every person who can read is reminded of that fact every day of his life and he believes it in a way, yet it does not become factual to him and enter his realization until he learns by experience its terrible truth.

We cannot escape the truth that everything in our lives rests entirely in our own hands; if we are not supreme in our own dominion and if we suffer, it is because we are not masters of that realm which is our very own and which we must eventually conquer, although it may take ages of experience to relate us in absolute mastery to our kingdom in our part of the divine life externalization.

True spiritual culture comes from the purification of the self, which is a perfectly practical process. It does not consist in prayer and fasting, nor yet in sackcloth and ashes, but in living a life of service, and the life of service is not only a life of continual experience and consequent development, but it is distinctly a life of joy.

The effect of any experience which has once made its impression upon the soul abides with it for all time, really becomes a storehouse of power, and may be utilized and drawn upon whenever occasion demands.

Human life ascends according to the increase of human consciousness, and with increasing consciousness we select grander and broader experiences as we pass from one association to another and one environment to another to meet the strengthening desire of the growing soul.

When we have perceived, as most of us do somewhere along our pathway, that we have not learned the lesson which our experiences should have taught us — instead of regretting the experience and feeling that had we done differently we might have escaped certain griefs, let us so relate ourselves to life in construction that we will only attract constructive experiences, and then they will not relate us to grief.

We find ourselves walking along sorrowful lines many times, because we fail to appreciate ourselves and give ourselves proper recognition; no man can be happy and do the good and beautiful thing unless he realizes that he himself is good and beautiful.

When we are conscious of our strength on any plane, we naturally live at the point of our highest realization. If I know that I am clever I shall live up to that cleverness, as it were, and do the clever thing. On the contrary, if I have a belief that I am stupid and that what I do is of no consequence, I shall very soon live stupidly and be stupid, because we attract exactly the sort of experience our quality demands and we get out of it just and justly what our capacity permits.

And men are not creatures of circumstance; their quality is the result of their desires; they are creatures of experience which responds to their desires, and their own desire is the magnet which attracts to them what they actually require for their development.

There are so many varieties in human expression; life becomes so vividly interesting as our experiences unroll, each one strengthening and beautifying and making way for another step in our newer and freer consciousness wherein our motive energy transcends our former intention in our life and in our work.

Indeed the true server of God, be he writer or painter, business man or home maker, is he who, through his holy motive, succeeds because his thought and his love are for and in his work rather than in and for the reward of the work.

When one's motive is outside of self, that is apart from greed and sense gain, and when his aim is toward some work of value to his race instead of toward some benefit or accumulation for himself, he cannot escape success, because it follows inevitably — but the moment the motive energy is degraded and its intentive force points, ever so slightly, toward money or fame or any other sort of personal possession, the work itself becomes degraded or lacking in magnetic power.

Men and women who are taking the position of leaders and teachers in the newer awakening, assume peculiar responsibilities, and they soon learn that they must make their statements from the knowledge which is based upon experience rather than belief, because every formulated thought, sent into the heart of an inquiring soul, reacts according to its motive force upon the person who formulated the thought.

All things and all activities have their place and their use in the Cosmic experience. As we are entering the consciousness of the next dimension it is well that we shall realize that we are actually and factually just what we have accumulated of the infinite experience and that all which is not accurate in our life accumulation shall pass into its original substance, for only intelligent goodness may prevail in the expressed idea of the ever-living God.

Nothing can interfere with the ultimate completeness of this universe; all manifest life shall be unified with the supreme good in that infinite and glorious intelligence. Already in the mind of the universe is this intention formulated, and it is now in process of externalization.

For ages has the universal mind taken the individual soul, which is the Ego, through many forms of its unfolding life experience; it has evolved through the mineral and vegetable and animal realms, not necessarily upon this planet, but somewhere in the Father's many mansions.

And now, you and I have come to the place where we are human creatures manifesting in the divine image, relating ourselves to God in conscious strength through our human experience.

Verily we shall prove ourselves worthy of our divine humanity.

STUDY OF WHY

To him that hath, shall all be given,
Because he has BECOME
The thing which he has claimed.

To him that knows, shall all be spoken,
Because he freely speaks
The truth he has attained.

For men become whate'er they claim,
And in the truth of being
And in the joy of giving,
Comes knowledge — vast and infinite
Of life unending.

Study of Why

GOD knows.

Therefore God is.

To know is to be and the whole of externalized life has become manifest or, it may be more accurate to say, is becoming manifest because of the knowledge of an infinite intelligence.

The human creature is externalizing himself according to his knowledge; he is in process of becoming whole, and each step in realization which adds to his knowledge renders him more complete and more wholly in his actual being. .

Knowledge is man's one and only possession; every other force and attribute in all nature and in all life leads toward knowledge, but until it becomes knowledge, it is not really and factually his own.

Knowledge is inclusive; its entire trend is toward wholeness.

Knowledge is good; therefore it is everlasting.

The innate demand of the soul, the true desire of the heart, the craving of the mind, and even the claim of the flesh is to know.

Know what?

To know what we are, who we are, from whence we came, whither we are going, and finally and primarily and most demandingly, WHY are we?

We have a vague consciousness that WE ARE because GOD is.

But it is very vague and so very much blurred by innumerable opinions and so dwarfed by fear that we almost have an idea that God is because we are.

WHY precedes the subtle query of the soul.

WHAT is the symbol of mental demand and precedes questions relating to information concerning facts and conditions and personality.

WHEN and WHERE are especially adapted to questions pertaining to physical expression and sense demands.

WHICH is entirely on the plane of discrimination or selection, which may, of course, be
applied to all realms.

How and HOW MUCH belong to the financial and purely external plane of expression, as spiritual forces cannot be weighed
and measured and the spiritual man soon forgets the plane of bargain measurements.

A person with a fair fund of information
can reply to almost any question commencing with WHAT —

To illustrate: What is the dominant color
of the earth planet when it is expressing its
life energy?

Ans.   Green.

That is not difficult; any person with eyes
to see can answer that.

But take the more subtle question.

Q. Why is the earth color green?

Ans. Because the earth planet is fourth in
the color spectrum of the solar system of which
it is a part, it vibrates in the tone of green
when it is most responsive to the universal
life current because green is the fourth color

visible to the human eye in its present development and in the direct order of its position in the spectrum — viz: Violet, Indigo, Blue, GREEN, Yellow, Orange, Red.

While that is a simple primary reply to a very commonplace question, you can easily see how much more subtle is the response to the query of WHY than to the more direct query of WHAT.

The man who is capable of formulating any question intelligently which commences with WHY is capable of answering that question, because the desire to analyze requires a cooperation of soul consciousness and mental effort which is a trifle beyond mere external fact, so unless the man has the capacity to answer it, whether he takes the trouble to do so or not, he has not the capacity to formulate it to the focusing point of asking some one else to do so.

And it is not always mental indolence which is our reason for seeking for causes outside of ourselves — rather, it is that so few people are aware of their own ability and of their

actual power. As a rule most folks are so
absorbed with non-essentials and with their
introspective worries which are connected
with their personality and their creature
comforts that they have almost lost their
appreciation of their God-given individuality
and their divinely innate strength and glorious opportunity.

Possibly we may think that it is of no real
use to understand this WHY of things — we
may feel that we have no connection with
universal causes and that anything which
does not concern our personal interest is none
of our affairs.

But if it is true, as most of us say we believe, that we are a part of the whole of infinite
life, surely we have some small share in its
causation as well as in its effect, and the fact
is that as soon as we lose our interest in
causes, effects become less vital in their relation to us and life becomes, therefore, less
interesting in our responsibility toward it
and we, less masterful in our intentive force.

And then what happens?

Can you not see it on every side? Indif-
ference, breeding all sorts of disease germs;
Selfishness, cultivating atrophication; Introspection, causing insanity; Graft and Greed,
attracting poverty and causing crime; and
all leading to the numbing of faculties and
the disseverance of the life current from its
vitalized center of universal action.

When we arouse to the realization that we
are a part of the infinite expression and a direct result of a divinely intelligent intention,
we not only have the ability but it becomes
our sacred desire to ask of the great cause —

Why am I?

Every attainment results from process.

Every accurate process emanates from some
intelligent cause.

Every force in operation is set in motion by
some primal power so related to it that it qualifies and vibrates with it with sufficient strength
of intelligent intention to give it impetus.

So nothing can be small and nothing can
be great in this vast universal process, because
it all proceeds from primal cause and all

operating in intelligent economy of nature's finer forces for the ultimate perfect expression of the whole.

And the smallest and weakest of living creatures is deeply concerned because he is the cause as he is the effect of his part of this marvelous universe.

And you and I are deeply concerned; according to the quality of our life energy and according to the degree of our universality, shall we answer and understand and know WHY we are alive in God's great home and WHY He in His supreme intention has included you and me.

The universe is in process and in expression because its creator and manifestor has given it Himself, His life energy, His love, and His wisdom.

You and I are in process and in expression because we are a part of that creator and manifestor and we are doing as much as we know because we are living as much as we know to unify and glorify and perfect the whole.

Life always expresses according to the knowledge of the being or the creature or the thing that is expressing it.

Why?

Because life is the activity of universal intelligence, and it can only vibrate through and with that intelligence which is the actual formulator of all manifestation.

A blade of grass expresses only in the degree of its consciousness; it is manifesting its degree of God's life and it gives and does as much as it knows.

The bird lives and is exactly what it knows; therein rests the truth of its being.

Men are alive at the point of their true knowledge, for life always advances to meet truth and knowledge is inevitably true or it is not knowledge.

God is the knower — His life is absolute law and truth is the evidence of Him and of the absolute eternal accuracy of that law.

Knowledge transcends all reason; it requires no proof and admits of no argument.

Men know far more than they are aware
that they know, but they understand far less
than they think they understand.

Why?

Because human understanding is the response of analysis and mental effort; it is
on the plane of reason and frequently answers
to argument and to opinion. It is largely
related to details of life and seldom goes
beyond personality.

Knowledge only responds to actual truth;
it has nothing to do with supposition or "say
so." Knowledge belongs to the plane of in-
stinct and inspiration and while it sometimes
follows understanding, it stands supreme in
soul consciousness as an actual revelation of
fact.

Humanity is measured by its own measurement. Each soul takes its own position in
earth life according to its own estimate.

Why?

Because each person has his own particular
and individual grasp of the universal mind;
he selects it by his desire and formulates it

by his intentive will, and he can increase it by his increasing desire and develop it by his more conscious will, or he may think around and around in the same little rut until he becomes too indifferent to reach out into universal mind at all and subsists on the small part he has already selected, and then it will follow as the night follows the day that he orders his life by somebody else's opinion and that his possessions are the result of some body else's creative energy.

. .

It is insolence for one person to presume to dictate the order of his life to another.

Why?

Because each soul must interpret life for itself. How can I tell of your requirements? What can I know of your desire? Am I greater than my brother that I should presume to decide his problem or to visualize for him the plan of his life?

Each soul's idea of God is his highest conception of himself.

Why?

Because no person can think beyond his capacity and no person can love beyond his ideal, neither can he judge of that which is not within his own mind.

If a man is afraid of the vengeance of God and sees in Him a personal embodiment of wrath, he himself must be vengeful in his thought and personal in his judgment. If, on the contrary, he sees the universe as God and sees love in its action, he is impersonal in His action and his ideals are constructive; naturally his life expression follows in natural, normal, and successful lines.

Anyone who makes a definite statement or asserts a principle, especially when he claims mastery of that principle, should be able to answer any query concerning it, as he should know the truth of anything he claims for himself.

Many a soul has lost a great opportunity by claiming that which he can neither use nor comprehend, but which having claimed, he must assume.

Why?

Because one of the privileges of humanity is to select its own opportunity and its own position in life.

A man may fulfil any desire of his body, his mind, or his heart if he is willing to pay the price; should he demand too much or assert himself beyond his strength, he must pay the price for that also.

. .

Wise indeed is he who can answer the "Why" of an inquiring child.

Why?

Because the child-mind is direct — and he who becomes as a little child is seeking the direct truth without fear and without limitation; the natural, normal child mind is not shadowed by fear and misunderstanding; it has not obscured its touch with the infinite mind by cramming its memory with non-essentials or by trying to get ahead of its friends and companions. So the child mind is a very clear medium for his soul demand,

and its questions are far more subtle than the supposedly wiser mind perceives.

There is a question in every mind and a longing in every heart concerning the truth of that living, loving God whose intimacy is our very own whenever we are sufficiently true to ourselves to be true to Him.

What does it matter to you and to me what else life reveals to us so long as we are close in the heart of a supreme omnipresent intelligence when therein nothing but good can remain? Nor can we remain in that sacred center unless we are true to it by living the chaste good, which is its life. And we shall know it in order to live it and by living it, to attract and to assimilate it until we become interpenetrated with the divine energy and all of life's love and wisdom is our very own.

But every possession carries its own responsibility, and knowledge, which is the greatest of all possessions, bears the responsibility in the demand of life that we live the truth that we know.

Never fear that you will not have the knowledge according to the strength of your desire and never doubt that you will have the power and the ability to express yourself according to your knowledge, for your strength comes according to the quality of your motive, and whether you express it in music, in oratory, in the domestic or social or commercial realm, or in any other form of art or science, the genius of you will reveal itself whenever and however you are ready and willing and awake to your own share in and of the God work.

Sometimes, in fact most times, it is wisdom to rest in the law of non-resistance.

Any man can force an issue, any man can act according to his will, but it takes a strong, trained soul to wait for his perfect hour.

The man who knows his work and his hour is great enough to be STILL and wait — he knows that in the actual being good, of being God-conscious, he is of far more value to the planet by giving it silently his great uplifting force than by all the enthusiastic shouting he can possibly do.

Overcoming may be superficial and rests with the emotions.

Becoming is actuality and includes the whole.

There is far more in actual being than in much doing, because being is unity with God force; it is deep and flawless and qualifies with every phase of constructive consciousness and of ultimate perfection.

. .

Onward Brother, —

The light is yonder, just beyond the fear line.

Only fear is to be feared, so move on out of its shadow into the light of your own faith and in the joy of your own work, that you may be alive and attuned to the goodness of your service.

Forgive your yesterdays; they have given strength and wisdom to your to-day.

Release them and let them go, that you may go forward in the path of a more vitalized service for yourself and for all else of God's beautiful, living things which need your faith and your strength and your love.

Lift up your eyes to the everlasting hills.

Reach out your arms to the star of your highest aim and sing the soul song of gladness that you are going forward in unity with life's intention and pray that your faith in its fulfilment may endure always.

WHOLE–NESS

In the strength of God's
  revelation
Do I manifest my life,
For in that revealing glory
His truth and His power,
His love and His wisdom
Are mine own.

And I am one with His
  free life
And one with His vast
  evidence
Of truth in whole-ness.

Whole=ness

HOLE.
Cosmic.
Complete.

The whole man is the divine man; he is cosmic in his consciousness and complete in his life expression.

The human creature is the divine creature in process; in other words, humanity is divinity in process.

The man is creating himself, and whether consciously or unconsciously, he is breathing into himself, with every inbreath he takes, the quality of the universal substance which he selects by the quality of his thought.

In the heart of him, this human creator intends to be whole; his innate desire is for the good of his part of life, which is health and money and joy and love and all else that is dear to the heart and flesh of mankind; not only does he desire this good, but he works for and toward it so long as hope sustains him, which is just as long as he realizes the good or the God of himself.

The only way that the thing we call evil can possibly exist is when good is ignored.

Ignorance darkens the light of truth and limits the activity of intelligence, so that when we ignore good, we create a lack in our whole-ness; we may call this lack sickness, we may call it poverty, indeed, we may term it sin, but whatever we name it, it is ignorance which has excluded some part of our good and we are not whole.

Ignorance does not mean lack of book learn-ing; many of God's children are so filled with the contents of books that they are fearfully and wonderfully ignorant, and some are so highly trained in militarism and other man-invented sciences that they ignore every law of God's humanity and human divinity.

Knowledge is necessarily good, because it is impossible to KNOW a thing which does not exist, and if men desire to be whole in the manifestation of their part of the infinite and intelligent life, they will seek with their hearts aflame and their minds alive for KNOWLEDGE, that they may not only be whole but wholly good.

Darkness is the nothingness of light as ignorance is the nothingness of consciousness and as fear is the nothingness of faith.

The easy way to dissolve the darkness is to turn on the light; it is an entire waste of energy to deny the dark, but whenever the shine of the light enters, we know there is no such thing as darkness; so no matter what form of disease the dark represents, whether sickness or any other sin symbol, just flash the truth light of love and faith therein before we claim there is no disease, because until we do dissolve it by our love and our faith there remains the symbol of the dark to our outer senses.

Love dissolves everything which we call evil; its interpenetrative subtleness casts out the shadow of the misinterpretation of good, and all the forces of human life activity are balanced in the light of the love shine.

It is quite possible that in the realm of our
untried strength there are cosmic forces
which far outreach our present unfinished
consciousness; the light of to-morrow may
utterly obscure the light of to-day; the shine
of a new dimension may entirely transcend
all that we now perceive.

We are quite as much in eternity now while
we are children of the earth home as we ever
shall be; God's life is enfolding us now as it
always has and as it always will; it is only
necessary that we desire to know God, which
means to know the good of ourselves, to actually be in heaven, because any soul who
know himself as he really is desires to live
his part of life in goodness that he may fulfil
the law of his soul desire.

The desire of the soul is always for completeness; its entire age-long journey is for
cosmic expression; step by step, life by life,
always learning, always adding to its wisdom
and to its love, this marvelous interactive
soul is involving and evolving in the intention
of becoming whole.

Each soul which has created for itself a body, whether an earth body or a sun body or any other body, is the microcosm of the universe from the angle of the home of that body; it has its own center and its own opportunity from that angle.

When the soul creates its spiritual body, which means its cosmic body, it has an infinite reach of consciousness and it evolves from the universal or cosmic realm of consciousness and is then one with the Father, ready to live and work and BE One with the Father in heaven or, in other words, One with divine harmony.

Most of the earth children are far from the place of divine harmony; they do not understand themselves and consequently cannot comprehend their fellow-men. We cannot possibly see in anyone qualities which are not in ourselves, and the more vitalized they are in ourselves, the more dominant they appear in others.

Which is the reason we are warned to judge not that we be not judged; those things which especially annoy us in other people are rampant in ourselves or we would not be disturbed by them, and it is much wiser to use the energy we expend in criticising other people in loving ourselves into harmony that we may help them onward by our faith and understanding rather than hold ourselves back and so intrude in the march of the race.

And no man and no condition and no complication of forces can interfere with the onsweep of life; we may resist Life's law, but if we do, it is you and I who will be crushed and broken; God's law knows only good, and when we are not good we are apart from THAT law.

It is the infinite variety of life which works in togetherness for completeness or wholliness — no two human beings of all the millions of all God's great humanity are alike, no two atoms in all nature are alike, nor do they occupy the same space — so the man and so the atom will work from their own individual center, the man relating himself and the atom relating itself to the whole universe from their angle of expression and not from

the viewpoint or from the desire angle of any
other point of consciousness.

Until the children of earth arrive at the
place of cosmic consciousness and become
divine, they are still human, and it is the wise
thing for them to balance in the place of their
humanity before claiming divinity.

To be humanly whole, the earth child will
express beauty and health and wealth and joy;
he will ignore no slightest detail which helps
to relate him to ease of flesh or peace of mind.

To be beautiful and wholly in flesh, we will
balance in beauty of mind; we will relate ourselves to the harmony of our part of the earth,
and we will be well groomed and well growned
and well mannered according to the demands
of our neighbors and our own soul call.

When we love our neighbors as ourselves,
we will love to please them and to serve them
as we love to serve ourselves — and our
neighbors are becoming nearer and dearer
and more numerous as modern life with its
travel and easy methods of communication
make more intimate our relationship.

To be healthy and wholly in our earth body, we will be at ease in our minds and kind in our hearts; then we shall be clean in our flesh and pure and sweet in our consciousness.

There is no greater asset in the health life than the purity of soul and mind which thinks goodness and speaks kindness.

Blessed indeed are the pure in heart.

If we would be wholly in the riches of earth, we will be free in our love for and in our use of the earth bounty; we will be unafraid that we shall lack at any point of our human expression.

God's money is our money when we know we are His children; the creature who actually knows he is interrelated with the universe, which means he is a child of God, has the right angle of relationship to the infinite and intelligent good.

Joy is one of the attributes of wholliness; who that is kind to his fellow-men and who obeys the highest dictates of his heart and mind can be otherwise than joyous?

· Ease is one of the attributes of wholliness;

it is a mistake to think that it is hard to be good and to follow what is called the path of righteousness.

To be good is the only easy way of being; any other state of being relates us to lack of ease which we call disease, and we can become uneasy in mind and diseased in flesh very quickly when we disconnect ourselves from good.

And righteousness is merely the right angle of consciousness which is our individual place of vision and our center in the infinite whole; when we follow the path of righteousness, we are true to ourselves according to our understanding and living right as our vision recognizes right.

There are no accidents in the all-life; every result has a cause somewhere along the way. The law of life is as accurate as the force of justice which sustains it, and justice is absolute because it is the exact right angle of all intelligent action.

If I so far forget myself as to judge and criticise and condemn my brother I am thereby creating a triangular force of judgment and criticism and condemnation which, when put in operation by my intentive energy, returns to the heart of me in the precise angle and ratio in which it was projected, and it reacts on my life forces according to the quality and force of my intention.

Is it surprising that some of us develop disease of the flesh and crinkle up in lines that men dread as signals of on-coming age?

There is no excuse for hideous flesh because of long life; time would mark us in beauty and wholliness if we would allow it, but we resist and hate and fear and fight, we put into action and create in the atoms of our flesh forces of destruction which lead to disintegration most ghastly. And then, afraid of the thing which we have done, we beg for mercy, thinking we may attract some special favor from God, whom we have dishonored and betrayed.

It is our privilege to free the Christ of ourselves from the Judas of our own heart center, that we may walk along our path of righteousness with clean hands and a pure heart.

We want to live according to our vision of the right angle of our part of life. We want to rest at the right hand of our God and we desire above all else that we only receive what we deserve.

And we intend to deserve by our work and by our love all of life's good in whole-ness.

There is ONE God.

That one God is the universal whole.

Uni-verse literally means One-whole, and in the Divine Unity is the primal substance externalized by one wholly principle and one infinite process.

The physical senses do not comprehend the externalization of life through the inbreath and outbreath of the omni-active God, — but the man who desires to KNOW concerning God and who intends to live in the good of the earth life can and does relate himself to the accurate action of the infinite intelligence — he then lives in the law, which means that he breathes with the activity of God, and in that divine breath the human creature is made whole.

We are never anxious when we are related to the law in the pure desire; it is only when we resist the law that we fail or fall.

This glorious law is mindful of its own and, like a wise and loving parent, it sometimes points the way in punishment and pain when the child it loves resists its perfect work.

Suppose our human brain does not quite understand; it can lay its burden on the law and wait until the way is made plain. When we trust, the waiting is not long or wearisome.

Suppose our will is thwarted and our desire suppressed; it is only that something is unfinished which we have left undone, some cause has tangled the thread of our accurate life action, and it is for us to finish and clear our path which leads to righteousness.

So we will breathe in our hearts for the beautiful light of construction, that it may show us the way to walk at ease along the righteous highway toward our Cosmic expression of whole-ness.

Nothing which we have assumed can be left unfinished; it is useless to attempt to escape from any force which we have once set in motion.

When the supreme intelligence breathes into the human creature the breath of life which is the Cosmic breath, he is then made or manifested in the image of God with the attributes of God, and he becomes his own creator, which really means his own externalizer; because there is nothing new in the universe, unmanifest, yes, and unexpressed — but every atom of cosmic substance, expressed or unexpressed, is waiting in its own time and place the awakening breath of God.

The atom must be complete before the man is whole.

The man must be complete before the race is whole.

The race must be unified in love and wisdom and complete in wholliness before its earth home manifests in perfection.

Verily there is nothing unworthy in God's great life, nothing to be ignored, nothing which may not be wrought anew and no problem which is not solved (saved) in the recognition of the divine human relationship of God and Man.

As yet the man creature is but an infant in consciousness; he writhes in his fierce unrest like the child which fights with all its puny strength the hand that guides it to safety.

It is good to know that time is endless and that good shall prevail.

Ay, though ages and ages roll away before divine unity is expresssed, God's children shall return to Him in whole-ness.

STUDY OF FREEDOM

'Tis not enough for me to say
That God is good.
No man can know of good
Least he is good.

'Tis not enough for me to speak
The word of life.
No man can know of life
Unless he lives.

Oh, heedless man — of mortal ken,
Thou knowest not
Of God and His intent
Until thou lovest all his life
And art alive thyself
Because of thy great love.

Study of Freedom

God make us free.
Hark ye to the cry of man,
God make us free —
From crushing unbelief in Thee
God make us free,
From grim, despairing pain and grief
God make us free.

Ah, pitying soul, dost thou not hear
Afar and near and everywhere —
From earth and sky and sea
Breathes out the prayer,
God makes us free.

Awake, O doubting heart,
'Tis only that thou did'st not know
That love is free,
That God is good and nothing else can be
When men are free.

How couldst thou know
That man is one with God,
One in His life and love,
One in His freedom?

It is not strange thy cry goes forth
In human discontent,
God make us free.

Arise, O man, and face thine own unfaith
And know that it has brought to thee
Thy pain and woe.

Know that from within thyself alone
Can shackles melt away
And freedom enter in, —
Know that 'tis thy lack, thy greed,
Thy fear and thy unrest
Which brands the heart of thee
And rends thy soul.

Oh, soul of love's intent, —
God make us free.

And it shall be.
The hour is nigh, the day is come,
The world awaits the call
Of men and angels
Who, all enthralled in God's great lovingness
Do know —
And knowing shall proclaim
God's world is free.

AFTERWORD

Afterword

A FAIR child stood at the gatway of a restless world.

Above her and around her and enfolding her was the fullness of a vivid life, and the child reached out her dimpling baby hand in gladness as she sang the beautiful song of youth: "It is all for me, for me — the great earth is my playground; the daisies bloom for me, and I shall sing and laugh and play always because of their love for me."

And the days rolled on and the fair child saw the daisies fade and the deep winter snows enfold her playground, while the bitter wind chilled the buoyant air and stilled the heart throb of the waters as it pressed them in its icy embrace.

A maiden stood at the threshold of life's temple of experience. "Never mind the fading daisies and the stilled waters," she sang. "I shall seek my joy in the throbbing heart of humanity; there I shall laugh and sing and play always because youth and beauty and love are all for me — for me, and I shall meet and conquer because of their love for me."

The days swept on and a woman with the flush of triumph on her face stood upon life's pinnacle. "O glorious life," she cried, "I love the fierceness of thy blast because I am greater than all its fury. I love thy great opulence because it is all for me — for me; and I love thy crashing torrent though it may sweep away all the world, it cannot assail me upon my pinnacle of fame and beauty and gold." And she raised high to heaven her slim white hands as though she would draw from its depths even more of earth's gifts to strengthen her triumph.

Even as the last tone of her exultant voice melted into the golden air, a shiver as of passing human agony swept over her swaying form and she stooped in shuddering surprise as a breath of fierce, anguished unrest entered her awakening heart and tore away all pride of flesh and gold and human adulations. And the woman saw as one aroused from a trance of ages a world teeming with struggling human creatures and herself one with them, no more no less than they.

The years blended into eternity and a woman, beautiful with the chastening glory of life's experience, stood out upon the sunlit plains while the radiance as of a great blessing fell around her gracious form. "O life," she cried, "at last I know thy law. I am created for thee, and as I give my love and my service to thee, all of thy great treasures are mine because I am created for thee —for thee, O glorious life!"

And, as the woman passed on into the mighty current of the world's work, she heard in the deep silence life's answer:

"O child, O maiden, O woman of sorrow and woman of joy, thou hast met me and learned my lesson well.

"My sorrows which thou hast overcome with love, my joys which thou hast welcomed with love, my labors which thou hast accomplished in love, have given thee this great

enlightenment, that love is the fulfilment of
my law; in that realization thou knowest
that no man can be greater than another and
no man can be lesser than another, humanity
is one in God's clear love.

"And thou shalt sing and laugh always
because of thy love."

THINK RIGHT

FOR

HEALTH AND SUCCESS

BY

GRACE M. BROWN

AUTHOR OF MENTAL HARMONY, ETC.

NEW YORK
EDWARD J. CLODE
PUBLISHER

FOREWORD

THE brightest of sunny days,
The bluest of soft warm skies
as a brilliant sun looked down upon
a group of men gathered about a wondrous
man with glorious love in his tender eyes
as he bent above them to impress his words
upon their hearts.

"As you think in your hearts, so are you,"
said he: — as you *think*, as you think in
your hearts.

And, while hundreds of years have passed
into infinite memories since that sweet sunny
day — although hundreds of teachers have
said again, "As you think in your heart, so
are you," — the day has not yet arrived
when men *know* that it is true and that they
truly become whatever they think in their
hearts.

Each soul has his own place in God's great
realm — each child has his own place in
God's earth home, and it is not an accidental

home nor an accidental place, no indeed —
it is the place which he creates for himself,
the home wherein his own thought has placed
him.

When the man thinks according to the
right angle of his earth position and when he
holds steady that position in the right angle
of his part of life, he attracts to himself all
that is good in universal life.

And the good of life is all that is worth
while in our being and in our living — health,
success, opulence, and happiness on all planes.

Verily there are no terrible life errors when
the man thinks within his own right angle of
life.

And never was a truer work spoken to
the souls of men than "As a man thinketh
in his heart, so is he."

To think the thought which appeals to you
Is to do the thing which is right for you.
To live the life which belongs to you
Means life's truth to you.

CONTENTS

We measure ourselves
By the quality of our thought,
By the strength of our desire,
By the purity of our love,
And by the accuracy of our selection.

Then let us know
That we become what we think,
That we do as we desire,
That we have what we love,
And that we manifest God's life as we select.

Therefore:
Let us qualify in truth,
Let us desire to do good,
Let us love God's treasures,
And let us select health on all planes
That we may measure ourselves in His Name.

Made in the USA
Coppell, TX
05 December 2020

43205093R00111